CONSERVATIVE EDITION

WHY WE'LL WIN

THE RIGHT'S LEADING VOICES ARGUE THE CASE FOR AMERICA'S TOUGHEST ISSUES

MALCOLM FRIEDBERG

SOURCEBOOKS, INC.®
NAPERVILLE, ILLINOIS

Published by Sourcebooks, Inc.
P.O. Box 4410, Naperville, Illinois 60567-4410
(630) 961-3900
Fax: (630) 961-2168
www.sourcebooks.com

Why we'll win-conservative edition : the right's leading voices argue the case for America's toughest issues / [edited by] Malcolm Friedberg.
p. cm.
ISBN 978-1-4022-0857-7
1. Conservatism–United States. 2. United States–Politics and government–2001-
I. Friedberg, Malcolm.

JC573.2.U6W5395 2007
320.520973–dc22

2007022748

Printed in Canada.
WC 10 9 8 7 6 5 4 3 2 1

To the men and women who have defended
the ideals on which this country was
founded . . . and to their parents.

"We all must recognize that we can disagree, we can debate, and we can continue to disagree . . . but this must not become hatred for another human being."

–President Ronald Reagan

In the spirit of former President Reagan, the Founding Fathers, and the principles upon which our nation was established, I encourage you to visit whywellwin.com and download (FREE of charge) the opposing views to those presented in this version of the book.

Contents

ACKNOWLEDGEMENTS

A good life is made up of contributions, some small and some not so small, by the many people who touch it. Once in a while we take the time to thank them. For those I've missed, thank you.

As for this particular project, there are several groups of people I would like to recognize. The first is the eight individuals who took some of their very limited and precious time to share their perspectives. They asked for nothing in return. To one and all, I appreciate your generosity.

The second group is the law school professors who turned what was a dying piece of grey matter (my brain) into something more formidable. They helped me get excited about these ideas, and this book is a direct result of their passion for the law. Of the forty or so, two are particularly deserving of extra recognition. First, Kevin Mohr at Western State University School of Law, who helped his first year contracts class rid the word "basically"–and all its synonyms–from our vocabulary. He explained that the law is about being precise, and "basically" has no place in precision. I'm not sure he'll like this book, but because of him the word "basically" does not appear anywhere between its covers. Second, Allan Ides, who allowed me to write several drafts of chapters as an independent study course while at Loyola Law School and mentored me throughout the process. A truly decent human being whose support and generous contribution of time went way beyond the call of duty. Thank you, professors.

The third group is all the others who contributed in some way to this work. My father, Errol Friedberg, provided valuable comments and insights and gave me much moral support. Thanks, Dad. I also thank my Mom, Sylvia Friedberg, and Tom Blaylock for their conscientious reading of drafts. Thanks to my illustrator, Mike Hollingsworth, for helping bring my ideas to life. A giant THANK YOU to my publisher, Sourcebooks, for the courage and vision to invest in a first-timer, and to my editor, Peter Lynch, for his guidance and helpful comments. Finally, though certainly not least of all, thanks to my agent, Laura Gross, for finding a home for my idea and putting up with me throughout the process.

Each one of us has a reason to get up in the morning. I have three. To my sweetheart, Amy, and my two little guys, Mason and Hayden . . . I love you the most.

AUTHOR'S NOTE

THIS BOOK IS NOT FOR LAWYERS; IT'S FOR REGULAR FOLKS.

I say that because the law is about precision, and this book is far too broad to be precise. Although it includes a tremendous amount of important and accurate information, I have chosen to present it in a way that makes it accessible to all. For those places where I have not adequately represented the law, an argument, or a position as accurately as a reader would like, my apologies.

This book was written over several years, so it is impossible for me to identify all of its sources. The original cases were the single most important source material, and most of the historical and background material comes directly from discussions within each case. On a very regular basis, I consulted the Holy Grail for writers, the World Wide Web. Where I referred to a specific body of information, I tried to indicate that to the reader. More often, I simply took a fact or two to help provide the reader with enough information to understand the issue being discussed.

The most frequently used web sources were: websites for all the organizations represented or discussed in this book, Legal Information Institute at Cornell University Law School, the U.S. Supreme Court site, Webster's Online Dictionary, and Wikipedia.com. My apologies if I did not credit someone where I should have done so.

Finally, I have omitted all citations and other legal references other than case names (which I have neither italicized nor underlined, as is customary). These can be easily found using your favorite search engine. Several other sources that I consulted include: Ides & May's Constitutional Law Individual Rights, Ides & May's Constitutional Law National Powers and Federalism, Garner's Black's Law Dictionary, Hall's The Oxford Companion to the Supreme Court of the United States, and Barron & Dienes's Constitutional Law in a Nut Shell.

For the record, I do not take credit for any of the ideas or arguments in this book–my goal was to simplify and transfer them to you. On the other hand, although several people read drafts of the book, I alone am responsible for its content.

FUNDAMENTAL RIGHTS PRIMER

WHY ARE YOU READING A PRIMER? GOOD QUESTION. Fundamental rights are at the center of a number of socially debated constitutional issues. In order to understand issues such as abortion, physician-assisted suicide, and same-sex marriage, it is important to understand how the U.S. Constitution and courts distinguish between fundamental and non-fundamental rights. Fear not. This is the only primer in the book, and it's brief.

Fundamental rights refer to the core elements of who we are as people . . . and what we are as a nation of laws. In describing fundamental rights, the U.S. Supreme Court uses phrases like "deeply rooted in our society," "one of mankind's basic civil rights," and part of "one's own concept of existence, of meaning, of the universe, and of the mystery of human life." The right to marry is a fundamental right. The right to have children is a fundamental right. So are the rights to free speech, a fair trial, and practicing your religion in the manner of your choosing. From a constitutional perspective they are the rights that are deemed most highly valued and worthy of protection in a society that is based on individual liberty. As a result, no government–federal, state, or local–can take them away (except in rare situations, but we'll discuss that in another chapter).

What are these rights? Where do they come from? Fundamental rights derive directly from the Constitution. They are rights that are either "enumerated" (a fancy word that simply means that they are specifically listed) or implied through other established rights. For example, the right to raise your children is not mentioned in the Constitution but is implied from the right to "liberty" that appears in the Fourteenth Amendment. Whether a right is listed or implied is not critical, because these rights are treated equally. What matters is whether or not a right is deemed fundamental.

For you visual learners: remember the food triangle from grade school? Well, here's the fundamental rights version:

THE HEIRARCHY OF RIGHTS

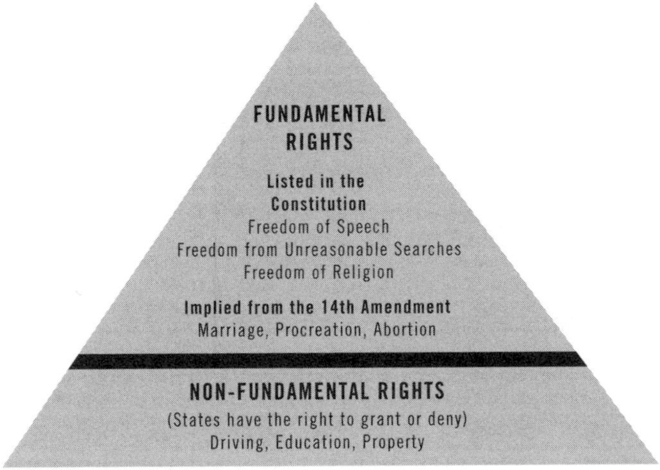
FUNDAMENTAL RIGHTS
Listed in the Constitution
Freedom of Speech
Freedom from Unreasonable Searches
Freedom of Religion
Implied from the 14th Amendment
Marriage, Procreation, Abortion
NON-FUNDAMENTAL RIGHTS
(States have the right to grant or deny)
Driving, Education, Property

Fundamental Rights Specifically Listed in the U.S. Constitution and the Bill of Rights

I am sure you recall the Bill of Rights (the first ten Amendments to the Constitution). The rights specified under the Constitution and the Bill of Rights–freedom of speech, freedom from illegal search, etc.–are guaranteed because they are listed in the Constitution. Those rights are absolute. The idea of losing these rights is not even open to debate. They are "inalienable" rights.

Fundamental Rights Implied by the U.S. Constitution and the Bill of Rights

What about other fundamental rights that are not expressly listed? Many years ago, the United States Supreme Court decided that the concept of "liberty" appearing in the text of the Fourteenth Amendment (" . . . no State shall deprive any person of . . . liberty") should be interpreted to include more than the rights specified in the Constitution. It did so because many fundamental rights, such as the rights to marry, have protected sex, and raise a family, are not listed. Thus, the Supreme Court determined that it was necessary to interpret the Constitution in a manner that upholds these rights (which are sometimes referred to as "privacy rights" or "basic rights"). As a result, these rights are implied through the concept of "liberty."

How Are Rights Implied?

Remember when you were back in high school, still under the rule of dear old mom and dad? Think of your parents as the law or, more specifically, as the Constitution. Some rights are explicitly granted to you. But your parents can't possibly list every specific thing you can and can't do, so some rights have to be implied. Let's assume that the right to drive the family car to a party on Friday night is a specifically granted right. On the way to the party, you stop to get some fast food. Although stopping for grub was not something your parents specifically stated you could do, it's probably still implied as a part of the right to drive the car that night. But let's say you get to the party and after an hour your best friend asks to borrow the car to go to another party. You're having a great time, so you tell him, "no problem, just be back by midnight." Under the parental law of "you can drive to the party," letting your friend borrow the car would *not* be implied from that law.

Non-Fundamental Rights: Not Protected by the Constitution, and the Decision of Whether to Protect the Right Is Made by Each State

If a specific right is neither listed in the text of the Constitution nor implied from the Fourteenth Amendment's idea of "liberty"(or from another established right) then it isn't protected by the Constitution. If it's not protected by the Constitution, then your state can deprive you of that right. Why? Because your state (really, the people of your state) has an interest in making its own decisions about what's important. For example, if the people of the State of California don't want its citizens to light fireworks on the Fourth of July because they are concerned about their state burning down, then it is perfectly reasonable for the State legislature to pass a law that outlaws fireworks. Why? Because the right to light fireworks is not a "basic" or "deeply rooted" fundamental right that is worthy of protection by the Constitution.

This all seems rational and straightforward. Some rights are listed; some are implied. If they are neither listed nor implied, then each state decides whether or not to protect them. But, here's the catch . . . it's not at all obvious which rights *should* be implied.

The Problem of Interpreting Fundamental Rights

How should the Supreme Court go about deciding which rights are fundamental and which are not? Those mentioned in the Bill of Rights are specified, so no problem there. And we might all agree that the right of heterosexuals to marry is fundamental (we'll get to the same-sex marriage issue in a later chapter). We probably also agree that the right to have sex, have children, and raise your own child should also make the list. But at some point we–as reasonable, intelligent people–are going to disagree. At some point we're going to run out of rights that we *all* agree are fundamental.

And that takes us to the heart of the problem . . . the farther we stray from the precise words of the Constitution, the more room there is for argument about which rights should be considered fundamental. That's why some Justices believe that the Supreme Court should *not* be in the business of interpreting what is and is not fundamental. Their position is that these decisions should be left to each state. As you read the chapters in this book that deal with fundamental rights, you might ponder where you stand on each issue–constitutionally protected right, or right better left to the states to decide?

Remember, we are just getting started, so if you are uncertain about which rights the Constitution protects, don't worry. In a few minutes you'll have it down pat.

What is important is that you are now sufficiently primed for our first hotly debated issue, abortion. And you will see that the critical question in the abortion debate, one that can only be answered by addressing which rights are fundamental, is not at all straightforward. Simply stated, the question is this: Is the right to have an abortion an implied, fundamental right that is–or should be–protected by the Constitution?

FUNDAMENTAL RIGHTS

Where's the line?

What qualifies a right as fundamental is not simple to identify. The Supreme Court describes these rights as part of our history, culture, and individual identity. But what makes one right fundamental and another not fundamental? Here's a concrete example about a father's fundamental rights relating to his child:

Michael H. v. Gerald D. (1989)

Michael H. sued to establish paternity of his daughter. Blood tests showed a 98.07 percent chance that he was the father. But California law did not allow paternity investigations that might be destructive to the child (and in this case the mother was married to another man). The Supreme Court upheld the law, deciding that a man who fathered a child with a married woman did not have a fundamental right protected by the Constitution. Result: Natural fathers do not necessarily have protected rights.

Stanley v. Illinois (1972)

Peter and Joan Stanley lived together off and on for eighteen years. They had three children but were never married. According to an Illinois law, when Joan died, the children became wards of the State and not of the biological father. The Supreme Court overturned the law, stating that although the law was intended to limit the rights of unsuitable fathers, there was no evidence that Peter was unsuitable. Result: Suitable fathers have fundamental (constitutionally protected) rights.

The Line

Here's where the Court draws this line: "When an unwed father demonstrates a full commitment to . . . parenthood . . . his interest in personal contact with his child acquires substantial protection . . . But the mere existence of a biological link does not merit equivalent constitutional protection."

Why It Is Important Whether or Not a Right Is Deemed "Fundamental"

All laws that infringe on a fundamental right must pass the highest legal standard: Strict Scrutiny. In comparison, laws that impact non-fundamental rights only need to meet the lowest standard: Rational Basis (a full description of the requirements of Strict Scrutiny and Rational Basis appears in the Affirmative Action chapter). Since fewer laws will pass the higher, more challenging standard, rights that are deemed fundamental receive greater protection. In other words, it is much harder for the government to justify infringing on those rights.

ABORTION

ABORTION IS POSSIBLY THE MOST CONTROVERSIAL AND socially divisive issue explored in this book. It requires us to reflect on who we are as individuals, and not simply where we stand on the issue. Regardless of your position, a thoughtful consideration of abortion inevitably raises questions about God, creation, and the miracle of life. It's no wonder that emotions are powerfully stirred by the abortion debate. Unfortunately, in the midst of all the passion the important legal issues are often overlooked. This chapter is not designed to alter personal opinions or change minds. But if your goal is to help people "see the light," understanding these pages will equip you to explain the basic legal issues behind abortion law.

> People are very sensitive about this issue, and they are understandably touchy about the words used to describe key terms. For example, some people are horrified by the biological creature in a woman's abdomen being referred to as a fetus, whereas others might be equally upset by referring to it as a person. Science calls it an "embryo" and, as it develops, a "fetus." The Court uses those words, as well as "potential life" and "developing young." The Constitution does not use any of these terms. With apologies to those that are offended, this book will use the term "unborn human" to refer to the life that exists within a mother's womb, and a "woman's right to bodily integrity" or "right to choose" to refer to the choice a woman makes in aborting a pregnancy.

One more thing–this chapter is intended to help you understand the central issue of abortion. There are many other important issues that directly and indirectly impact a woman's right to choose and a state's right to protect the unborn. It is not practical to try and address all of these issues. Despite that, here's a sampling of what states can and cannot do in regulating abortion:

1. States can require parental notification for minors, although the minor must be provided with an opportunity to appear before a judge to obtain a waiver that would free her of this requirement. Conversely, if the minor chooses to have the child, there is no notification requirement.
2. States are not allowed to require a woman to obtain consent from the father in order to procure an abortion.
3. States have the option of whether or not to use public funds for abortions.
4. States can place restrictions on where abortions can be performed.
5. States can create mandatory waiting periods (24–48 hours) between the time the woman is first seen in a clinic and the time the procedure is performed.

Two basic questions must be examined to properly understand the abortion debate.

Question One: Does the Constitution protect a woman's right to have an abortion?

Question Two: If the Constitution protects a woman's right to an abortion *and* a state's right to protect the unborn, how should our legal system strike a fair balance between these two competing interests?

Question One:
Does the Constitution Specifically Protect a Woman's Right to Bodily Integrity During Pregnancy–to Choose Between Birthing a Baby and Aborting a Pregnancy?

Simply stated: No, it does not. The Constitution does not expressly protect a woman's right to an abortion. You could read the Constitution a thousand times and you would not find any words that mention abortion or a woman's right to choose. But the Constitution also does not protect a number of other rights we take for granted. For example, the Constitution says nothing about the right to be married or how many children you can have, or, quite surprisingly, an absolute right to vote. Since the right to have an abortion is not specified, it must be implied from another right in order for it to be protected. Roe v. Wade, the original case to tackle this issue, determined that abortion was an implied right (from the Fourteenth Amendment's idea of "liberty"). Let's take a moment to examine some important aspects of this historic and highly contentious case.

Roe v. Wade: Abortion Is a Fundamental Right

Since the Supreme Court's ruling in Roe v. Wade (1973), the law of the land is that a woman's right to abort a pregnancy is a fundamental right. In Roe, Ms. Jane Roe (see below for a piece of her story) challenged a Texas State law that made it a crime for a doctor to perform an abortion, punishable by two to five years of breaking rocks in the Texas heat. Roe challenged the law because she felt that the law limited her constitutional right to have an abortion (the argument being that if doctors were punished, most would not provide abortions with the practical result that abortion would be outlawed). In case you need a reminder, Ms. Roe won her case.

From What Right Was Abortion Implied?

If you are wondering how the Court implied abortion, give yourself a star. The answer is it was implied from the right of "privacy." One earlier case (Griswold v. Connecticut, 1965) dealt with a state's attempt to limit the distribution of contraceptives. In Griswold, the Court pointed to various established legal principles that they felt supported the existence of a personal "zone of privacy." In Roe, the Court picked up on this idea of privacy and determined that abortion fell within this zone.

In case you didn't notice, a "zone of privacy" is pretty vague. Even today, it remains unclear what this right entails and how it should be applied. Is the zone a physical area of bodily privacy? Or does it apply strictly to bedroom matters? How about privacy of personal information? Or the privacy rights of free association or freedom of thought?

On the one hand, the idea of personal privacy appears to make sense. However, the lack of a clear definition of this broad idea of privacy or "bodily autonomy," and what it entails, provides ammunition for the critics of abortion. And since the right to an abortion is implied from this right of privacy (which, in turn, is implied from the idea of "liberty"), this is where the argument that abortion is not a fundamental right begins.

Roe happened over thirty years ago. There were two primary people involved in the case: Jane Roe, the woman seeking to have an abortion, and Sarah Weddington, the lawyer who represented her.

Fast-forward to the present, and here is a small insight into how that event impacted their lives:

Jane Roe was the name the Court used to protect the identity of Norma McCorvey in Roe v. Wade. This is an excerpt from a book about her post-Roe experience, *Won by Love*, published in 1998:

"When I reached Pastor Sheats, I saw Jesus in his eyes. It made me feel so incredibly sorry for all my sins, especially for my role in legalizing abortion. I just kept repeating over and over, 'I just want to undo all the evil I've done in this world. I'm so sorry, God. I'm so, so sorry. As far as abortion is concerned, I just want to undo it. I want it all to just go away.' Finally, I stopped crying and broke into the biggest smile of my life. I no longer felt the pressure of my sin pushing down on my shoulders. The release was so quick that I felt like I could almost float outside."

Sarah Weddington was the young lawyer who argued Roe v. Wade on Norma McCorvey's behalf before the Supreme Court. This is an excerpt from her book, *A Question of Choice*, published in 1992:

"Three scenes summarize my life . . . First, a triumphant young woman, five years out of law school, celebrating the victory of a Supreme Court case she has won, Roe v. Wade, which overturns Texas anti-abortion statutes and makes abortion legal throughout the United States. Second, a worried mature woman, two decades later, writing and speaking with every ounce of energy to prevent what she hoped and believed American women would never again know: the horrors of a time when abortion was illegal . . . But there is also a third scene for me, one I share with millions of women: A scared graduate student in 1967 in a dirty, dusty Mexican border town [going] to have an abortion, fleeing the law that made abortion illegal in Texas."

In the Roe decision, the Supreme Court attempted to strike a balance between the interests of the woman and those of the state. For the woman, the Court recognized that the right to make the choice about whether or not to have a child is a fundamental right that falls within the definition of liberty. Therefore, it was protected by the Constitution. The Court also recognized that the state had a valid interest in protecting the unborn by promoting childbearing over abortion when the fetus became viable (after the second trimester).

The challenge was striking the *right* balance. And that brings us to Question Two . . .

Question Two:
How Do We Balance the Rights of the Mother with Those of the State (Acting on Behalf of the Unborn Human)?

The Roe Court adopted several key concepts about pregnancy and the law and fitted them neatly into a trimester system:

Trimester 1: The state cannot pass any regulation relating to abortion. None.

Trimester 2: The state can only pass regulation that relates to the mother's health, such as establishing qualifications of who can perform an abortion, where it can be performed, and the required licenses.

Trimester 3: The state's right to protect an unborn human begins after "fetal viability," the time after which the fetus can survive outside the mother's womb. After that "compelling point," the state can advance its interest in promoting life by regulating abortion. The only exception is when an abortion is necessary for the "health of the mother."

Roe stood for almost two decades. But those nineteen years brought many challenges and two new Justices to the Supreme Court. In 1992, the Court re-examined this issue and decided that there was a better approach to balancing the competing interests of a woman's choice and protecting the unborn human.

Definition of "Health of the Mother"

"The medical judgment may be exercised in light of all factors—physical, emotional, psychological, familial, and the woman's age—relevant to the well being of the patient. All these factors may relate to health." (Doe v. Bolton, 1973). In other words, the mother's health exception includes factors other than purely physical health.

The New Approach: Planned Parenthood v. Casey

In Planned Parenthood v. Casey (1992), the State of Pennsylvania passed a law that attempted to regulate other aspects of the abortion process, (for example, minors had to inform their parents and married women had to inform their husbands). The non-profit organization Planned Parenthood sued the State and its Governor, Mr. Casey, because it believed that the law violated Roe. In its decision, the Supreme Court kept some and scrapped other parts of Roe.

What Stayed

- A woman has a right to choose an abortion without undue interference from the State.
- Abortion rights are absolute prior to fetal viability.
- The State has a right to promote birth over abortion.

What Went

- The trimester system approach to determine when and how states can regulate abortion.

What's New

- The Undue Burden test to determine which state laws regulating abortion are constitutional and which are not, which can be applied at any stage of the pregnancy.

In its Casey decision, the Supreme Court recognized that the strict limitations of Roe's trimester system prevented states from taking legitimate steps to further their interest in protecting fetal life. But the Court was deeply divided on how to fix Roe, with several members wanting to abandon it, several wanting to keep it, and a few others wanting to redesign it. Despite this split, enough of a majority existed to realign the balance. As a result, states were given more flexibility in protecting the life of the unborn without totally compromising a woman's ability to seek an abortion. Roe's rigid trimester approach was gone, and it was replaced by a new standard that could be applied at any point in the pregnancy. That standard is the "Undue Burden" test.

Undue Burden Test

Simply put, the Undue Burden test says that an abortion law is unconstitutional if it creates an undue burden on a woman's right to choose an abortion. The obvious immediately following question is what constitutes an undue burden? In Casey, the Court interpreted an undue burden as simply a "substantial obstacle." What's a substantial obstacle? It's something that "prevents a significant number of women from having an abortion."

Some members of the Court were highly critical of the Undue Burden test. Compared to the rigidity of the trimester approach, the Undue Burden test made the law *more* difficult to define. Is an undue burden simply a little bump in the road? Or is it a more substantial hindrance? How about a total barrier? As a consequence of this uncertainty, this test provides little direction for states looking to adopt abortion legislation that is consistent with the Constitution. To paraphrase one Justice, it appears that any state legislation that is successful in decreasing the number of abortions would probably be considered an undue burden simply because of its success.

Only a single Supreme Court case has applied the Undue Burden test. Eight years after Casey was decided, in Stenberg v. Carhart (2000), the Supreme Court examined a Nebraska State law that made one type of abortion illegal: partial-birth abortion. The legal issue in Stenberg was whether or not the Nebraska State law that made it illegal to perform the partial-birth method of abortion was an undue burden. The Court primarily focused on medical evidence suggesting that there are times when a doctor may feel compelled to use this method to preserve the health of the mother. The Court determined that since the law did not allow a doctor to perform a particular type of abortion that might in some instances be the safest, the law indeed created a "substantial obstacle to a woman seeking an abortion." In other words, it was an undue burden. The Supreme Court deemed the Nebraska law unconstitutional.

Conclusion

And that's where we stand today. Abortion is protected by the Constitution, but a state can create laws to promote life . . . provided those laws do not present a substantial obstacle to a woman seeking an abortion.

On a political level, the debate about abortion is as intense as ever. In federal and state court nominations, it appears to be a critical factor. With voters, it is probably the best example of the "one-issue voter," in which individuals vote for a candidate solely on their stance on abortion.

A number of states have passed laws that directly conflict with the Roe and Casey decisions. For example, in 2006, South Dakota made it a crime for doctors to perform abortions except to save the mother's life. The specifics of the law are not as important as the apparent purpose for which these laws were passed . . . to create an opportunity for the Supreme Court to overturn Roe and Casey. (In South Dakota, the law was defeated in a statewide general election.)

In 2003 President Bush signed a federal ban on partial birth abortion; (the Partial-Birth Abortion Ban Act). The Supreme Court will rule on that law (Gonzalez v. Carhart) in 2007. For an update on the most recent developments involving these issues, please check the website at whywellwin.com.

Footnote

Partial-birth abortion (PBA) is a non-medical term that appears to describe several types of medical procedures. Explaining the details of PBA is beyond the scope of this book. To obtain different perspectives I recommend several websites including the National Right to Life (nrlc.org), Planned Parenthood Federation of America (plannedparenthood.org), and Wikipedia (wikipedia.org).

The methods described in Stenberg are graphic, no matter which side of the abortion debate you take. The dissenting opinion describes in great detail the ways in which an unborn human is removed from a woman and terminated. I don't recommend that most people suffer through a legal opinion, and this book is intended to save you that trouble by giving you the distilled version.

But if you are passionate about this issue and want to understand one medical procedure used in an abortion, you might be interested in two short paragraphs of the dissenting opinion of Justice Kennedy (Page 958, Section 1, paragraphs 3 and 4).

ESSAY

Dr. Wanda Franz

President, National Right to Life Committee

We hold these Truths to be self-evident, that all Men are created equal, that they are endowed by their Creator with certain unalienable Rights, that among these are Life, Liberty and the Pursuit of Happiness–That to secure these Rights, Governments are instituted among Men, deriving their just Powers from the Consent of the Governed . . .
–The Declaration of Independence, July 4, 1776

Consider the above words, and this is what we learn:

The right to life is a "self-evident truth"; it is not based on the feelings and shifting opinions of men.

The right to life is "unalienable" and an essential part of us. It exists independently from what others want. It is not a grant from government. It exists, whether there is a government or not. And it certainly can't be ruled out of existence by unelected judges.

The government derives its "just Powers from the Consent of the Governed," namely us. The Founding Fathers believed in "the capability of a people to govern themselves," as Abraham Lincoln put it.

The reason for government is "to secure these Rights." So the Constitution is, to use the words of political scientist Paul Rahe, the "instrument for the implementation" of the Declaration of Independence. Thus, judges are not free to ignore the principles laid down in the Declaration of Independence.

A look at the major abortion cases provides a litany of the Court majority's contempt for the Declaration of Independence.

Roe v. Wade and Doe v. Bolton (1973). The child in the womb is not "created equal," but receives effective legal rights only *after* birth. There is no "unalienable right to life," nor is that right a "self-evident truth." Instead, we have the feelings of the mother. As "pro-choice" columnist Ellen Goodman put it: "*We call* [the unborn child] *a baby when it's wanted and a fetus when it isn't.*" Indeed, in the world of Roe and Doe, a pregnant woman can schedule an abortion, change her mind tomorrow and plan on having the baby, and then change her mind again and have the abortion. In that world there is no place for the right to life as an unchanging and inherent attribute of a human being.

Doe goes even further than Roe: An elastic "health" exception provides the cover for any abortion. And the abortionist, once considered a most disreputable individual, has now, in the words of Justice Harry Blackmun, "the room he needs to make his best medical judgment." The self-evident truth about abortionists is, of course, that in their "best medical judgment" there is no unalienable right to life.

Do the Roe and Doe decisions represent "just Power" based on "the Consent of the Governed"? No. Dissenting Justice Byron R. White denounces them as "an exercise in raw judicial power." Do the decisions respect the constitutional framework of federalism and the separation of powers? No. "The people and the legislatures of the fifty states are constitutionally disentitled" with regard to abortion (Justice White). Is there a right to abortion in the Constitution, the "instrument for the implementation" of the Declaration of Independence? No. "The Court simply fashions and announces a new constitutional right for pregnant mothers" (Justice White).

In Roe and Doe, the Court dealt us two devastating blows: one to the individual human being–there is no unalienable right to life–and one to the whole republic–an oligarchy, the Court's unelected majority, now makes the law of the land.

Planned Parenthood v. Casey (1992). With neither the ability nor the willingness for resolving the legal and constitutional crises of its own making, the pro-abortion Court majority demands that we accept its miscarriage of justice; because for the Court to overrule "Roe's central holding" would "seriously weaken the Court's capacity to exercise the judicial power" and do "damage to the Court's legitimacy," even "if error was made." What we have here is a stubborn judicial oligarchy, willfully oblivious to its constitutional duty and filled with contempt for "the Consent of the Governed."

Stenberg v. Carhart (2000). The extreme nature of the Court's abortion rulings is now clear for all to see: With the excuse of "health" reasons, the abortionist may deliver a child–except for the baby's head–force a cannula into the base of the skull, and suck his brains out. Rather than securing the "unalienable right to Life and the Pursuit of Happiness," the Court is now shielding the butchers profiting in the bloody traffic of "choice." The Constitution, the "instrument for the implementation" of the Declaration of Independence, is now revoltingly perverted into a tool for its denial.

Thomas Jefferson worried about men making the Constitution into "a mere thing of wax in the hands of the judiciary, which they may twist and shape into any form they please." We have arrived at that point. And Abraham Lincoln warned us "that if the policy of the government, upon vital questions, affecting the whole people, is to be irrevocably fixed by decisions of the Supreme Court . . . the people will have ceased, to be their own rulers, having to that extent, practically resigned their government, into the hands of that eminent tribunal."

The radicalism of abortion law and its calamitous consequences motivate some to offer soothing calls for moderation and the "middle ground." Yes, abortion is bad, they say–though we are never told why–but they are for "choice." Or we ought to make abortion "safe, legal, and rare"–a clever, but nonsensical proposition. Make, let's say, embezzlement "safe and legal" and see how "rare" it becomes. The idea is even more absurd in the case of abortion. With its abortion decisions the Court created a whole new industry–an industry that has no interest whatsoever in making abortion "rare."

Of course, abortion *is* bad beyond the killing of the innocent. On an elementary level, the loss of labor force will reduce the gross national product and endanger our pension and transfer payments by 2020 (Lawrence Roberge, 1995). Completing one's first pregnancy reduces the risk for breast cancer, because immature breast cells are stimulated into differentiation and proper development. In contrast, an abortion interrupts that process and raises the likelihood of developing breast cancer (Joel Brind *et al.*, 1996). Women who abort are more apt to develop various forms of substance addiction (David Reardon *et al.*, 2004). In the California Medi-Cal program, women who aborted were 62 percent more apt than those having deliveries to die from suicide, accidents, AIDS, circulatory disease, cerebrovascular disease, and other heart disease (David Reardon *et al.*, 2002). They were significantly more likely to make Medi-Cal claims due to mental diseases (Patricia Coleman *et al.*, 2002; David Reardon *et al.*, 2003). Other studies suggest that children born to women who abort, compared to those who carry their pregnancies to term, are at higher risk of receiving less emotional support from their mothers and of having more behavioral problems (Patricia Coleman *et al.*, 2002). In addition, these children are at higher risk of being physically abused (Patricia Coleman *et al.*, 2005).

The legalization of abortion–in practice, abortion for any reason–has not only victimized millions and millions of individuals (over 45 million unborn children aborted since 1973, their mothers, and their kin); it has also corroded the soul of the whole people: Innocence is no longer a legal shield against being willfully killed. A child with a disability is in danger of suffering a "retroactive" abortion. The physically and mentally damaged may be denied food and water–"because she didn't want to live this way," so says someone in power who makes his own values supreme or has a conflict of interest. There is the right to physician-assisted suicide in Oregon, and there is pressure for euthanasia. Creating embryos and killing them for their stem cells is the latest demand for those who think nothing of conducting fatal experiments on fellow human beings. And, of course, in spite of the pernicious slogan "every child, a wanted child," child abuse is worse than ever. Human life has become cheap. Indeed, in accepting abortion we not only declare the unborn child to be worthless, we render the same judgment about ourselves.

STEM CELL RESEARCH

LABORATORY BABIES? HUMAN BODY PART FACTORIES? A new version of your dead dog? This chapter will attempt to demystify a few of the issues about stem cell research and its relationship to the law. Unfortunately, it will likely raise as many questions as it answers, because stem cell research is very new and its potential has yet to be established. Parkinson's disease, diabetes, cancer, heart disease, and many other afflictions are prime examples of diseases that *might* someday be cured using stem cell technology. But to what extent, and when, that potential will actually be realized is not clear at this time.

Despite these uncertainties, even critics agree that stem cells offer tremendous promise for curing certain diseases. That's why the debate is not about whether scientists *should* be doing stem cell research; rather, it is about the *source* of the stem cells.

> Stem cell research does not present a constitutional issue. Most scientific research is probably protected under the First Amendment right to academic freedom. I say probably because there is little case law on scientific research. So, why is it in this book? Because it is so closely connected to the abortion issue, and to the more fundamental question of when life begins, that it begs to be considered . . . think of it as a postscript to the abortion debate.

BIO 101: The Quickest Biology Lesson Since High School Science Class

The billions of cells in your body comprise about 220 specific cell types. Each cell type is structurally different and serves a unique function. Some cells pump your blood (muscle cells in your heart), some fire the impulses in your brain and spinal cord that enable you to feel and think (neurons), and others fight infections (white blood cells). The problem is that, with only a few exceptions, most cells in an adult reproduce ("replicate") either very slowly or not at all. So, if you lose your liver cells due to disease, injury, or drinking, there simply are no new cells to replace them. That's where stem cells come into the picture.

Stem Cells

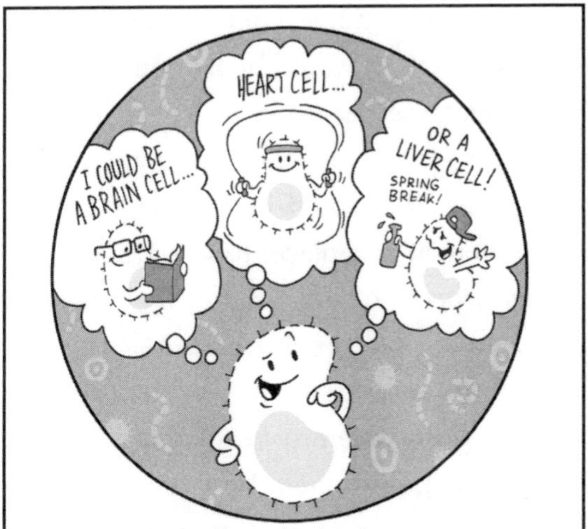

DREAMS OF A YOUNG STEM CELL

Stem cells are generic ("undifferentiated") cells that have the ability to turn into any of the 220 types of specialized cells in the body. (Because of this feature they are referred to as "pluripotent.") These generic cells can become brain cells, lung cells, or any other type of cell. Think of them as the body's equivalent of universal gold bars that can be changed into U.S. dollars, European euros, Japanese yen, or any other currency.

Suppose that you suffer from hepatitis or alcoholism that leads to permanent impairment of your liver function, or you get in a car accident and are paralyzed because the damage is so severe that your muscles can't function. Since your body will not make more of these cells, it would be helpful if there were a way to replace the damaged cells with new healthy ones (exchange some of those gold bars). Like a universal currency that could be exchanged, stem cells offer the potential to replace these lost liver or muscle cells. This process of exchanging or replacing stem cells is called "replacement therapy."

That's a brief description of what stem cells do. You don't have to be a scientist to see that if they live up to their potential, they could be a very important part of curing all types of disease. But the potential of stem cells isn't the source of the debate. Rather, the controversy about stem cell research is where and how scientists obtain them.

Sources of Stem Cells

Stem cells come primarily from two sources: human adults and human embryos. Adult stem cells do not have the ability to grow into a complete human being. Thus, using adult stem cells does not create an ethical dilemma. But some experts claim that adult cells may not be useful for replacement therapy. Consequently, they want to undertake stem cell research using the second source of stem cells . . . and that's where the debate begins.

The second source of cells is embryonic stem cells, which come from . . . you guessed it, human embryos. And if you believe that life begins at conception, then research on embryos is equivalent to research on human beings. And, obviously, that presents a problem.

There are four primary sources for embryonic cells:

1. Existing stem cell lines: One of the capabilities of stem cells is that they can regenerate or reproduce endlessly. The process of regeneration creates a "cell line." Although there were initially seventy established lines in existence, the actual number still around is up for debate and may be as few as twenty-two. Additionally, there is debate among experts about the usefulness of these remaining stem cell lines.
2. Cloned embryos: When a woman's egg is fertilized with a man's sperm, it creates a one-cell organism ("zygote"). That one cell divides into

two, four, eight, and eventually many millions of cells until it becomes an embryo (and later a fetus, and then a child). This embryo can be copied ("cloned"). Scientists are able to harvest embryos at the four-cell or eight-cell stage and remove an individual cell, which can (sometimes) grow in the laboratory as a new stem cell line.

3. Aborted or miscarried fetuses/embryos: When a fetus or embryo is aborted, either because of medical necessity or a woman's choice, stem cells can be removed from the aborted fetus/embryo for scientific research.
4. Unused IVF embryos: When a woman goes through IVF (*in vitro* fertilization), multiple eggs are removed from her uterus and fertilized. At least two fertilized eggs are placed back in her uterus (which is why women who have been through this procedure often have multiple births). Once the woman is pregnant, the unused fertilized embryos can be frozen for future procedures. If these stored embryos are not needed for further IVF procedures, they may be discarded or donated for research purposes.

It is important to recognize that there is significant debate among scholars as to the best source of stem cells. Some claim that adult cells or those from existing stem cell lines are adequate for research. Other scientists claim that cloned, aborted, or unused IVF cells should still be used because they offer greater potential.

Among laypeople, there are several different perspectives. In one significant way, stem cells mirror the abortion debate. If you believe that life begins at conception, then you are probably against embryonic stem cell research. However, you might believe that life begins at conception, but may be more open to research with unused IVF embryos (assuming they will be discarded) or those derived from clones (since they are manufactured and removed long before an embryo has formed), because there is no chance that these cells will develop into a human. Finally, you might believe that life does not begin until later in the development process (say, at least until the embryo has developed into a fetus), and thus are supportive of using embryonic stem cells regardless of the source.

Current Federal Law

Probably the most notable aspect of federal law in the area of stem cell research is that there isn't much. In

2001, the federal government banned the use of federal dollars on embryonic stem cell research for stem cell lines that were created after August of 2001–meaning that federal funding can only be used for the seventy (or twenty-two) existing stem cell lines. As a result, scientists are not permitted to use federal funds (usually in the form of grants from the National Institutes of Health or other federal agencies), nor to use equipment that was purchased with federal monies for research conducted on other stem cell lines. As a consequence, the only way to perform research on embryonic stem cells is with private (non-federal) funding.

The ban on funding is important because federal dollars are presently the largest and most firmly established source of support for scientific research. According to those who believe that research should not be limited to adult and existing stem cell lines, the lack of federal funding for embryonic cells will make it difficult for the United States to compete against foreign research in stem cell technology.

President Bush has not shied away from confronting the issue of stem cell research. In remarks he delivered to the nation on August 8, 2001, at the time his administration decided to restrict funding to existing stem cell lines, he identified the two competing considerations that are at the core of this conflict:

"As I thought through the issue, I kept returning to two fundamental questions: First, are these frozen embryos human life, and therefore something precious to be protected? And second, if they're going to be destroyed anyway, shouldn't they be used for a greater good, for research that has the potential to save and improve other lives? At its core, this issue forces us to confront fundamental questions about the beginnings of life and the ends of science. It lies at a difficult moral intersection, juxtaposing the need to protect life in all its phases with the prospect of saving and improving life in all its stages."

Sticking to his guns, when Congress passed the Stem Cell Research Enhancement Act of 2005 that amended the 2001 funding restrictions, the President used his veto power. That situation will likely present itself again in 2007 with the introduction of a new Congress and renewed momentum to fund embryonic stem cell research. In addition to the congressional efforts, states are getting in on the act by providing money for research. With a high concentration of biotech and venture capital firms, California was the first to act–and at the time of this writing, New York was also moving in that direction.

California's Big Investment

In 2004, California voters passed the California Stem Cell Research and Cures Bond Act (Proposition 71), which amended the State constitution. Prop. 71 established a $3 billion State fund to provide for stem cell research over a ten-year period. Prop. 71 is a direct attempt to address the lack of federal funding. Sponsored by various interests, most notably the biotech research industry and venture capital firms in California, Prop. 71 is not without its naysayers. Critics argue that it will be overly costly (interest payments on the debt will double the price tag from $3 billion to $6 billion), and they point out that the effectiveness of such research has yet to be established. Currently, Prop. 71 is being challenged in the California court system as a violation the State constitution. Stay tuned, as litigation will likely be resolved in 2007 or 2008.

Conclusion

This debate, like the technology that has spawned it, is relatively new. But it is one that is not going away. In fact, as the science improves the debate is only going to become more and more intense. As research on stem cells progresses, new ethical issues are likely to emerge, pushing the controversy beyond stem cell research. As we explore these new frontiers, we will be forced to examine ethical questions about what society should and should not be doing. Like it or not, the once far-fetched scenario of whether man is "playing God" by engineering cells or using other scientific techniques to improve our way of life may be a real question that your not-so-distant-future relatives will probably face. Stem cells are just the tip of the iceberg, and it is one issue that should spark questions about where and how we draw the lines in using our newfound knowledge.

ESSAY

Dr. Tom Coburn

U.S. Senator, Oklahoma

As a practicing physician and two-time cancer survivor, I have both a personal and professional interest in developing cures for diseases. However, I believe the American people need a second opinion on the potential benefits of destructive embryonic-stem-cell research. A bill put before in the Senate several terms ago, for the first time, directed the federal government to use taxpayer dollars to destroy human embryos.

This proposal was likely based on a false hope. Not a single treatment has been developed from embryonic stem cells, yet sixty-five treatments have been developed from stem cells in umbilical-cord blood and adult tissues.

Leading proponents of research on embryonic stem cells are themselves lowering expectations that dramatic cures to diseases such as cancer and Alzheimer's are just around the corner. The *Guardian* newspaper recently reported that Lord Winston, the most prominent embryonic-stem-cell researcher in the United Kingdom, said that hopes for cures had been distorted by arrogance and spin. "I view the current wave of optimism about embryonic stem cells with growing suspicion," Winston told the British Association for the Advancement of Science.

Similarly, South Korean cloning expert Curie Ahn now warns that scientists won't be able to develop cures from embryonic stem cells for three to five more decades. In experiment after experiment, scientists are learning that embryonic stem cells are too carcinogenic or "wild" for therapeutic purposes. For example, it is not uncommon in experiments on mammals for the animals to be killed by exotic tumors. In some cases, embryonic stem cells have triggered hair and bone growth inside the brains of subjects.

Meanwhile, astonishing breakthroughs are enabling scientists to use non-destructive techniques to develop pluripotent stem cells. (Pluripotent stem cells, like embryonic stem cells, have the ability to develop into any tissue in the body.) Harvard scientists recently converted human skin cells into pluripotent stem cells without destroying a human embryo in the process. Every other useful stem-cell therapy developed so far has not required the destruction of human embryos. Science is demonstrating that we will likely arrive at the same destination–and cures–without needing to go down the path of taxpayer-funded research that destroys human life. I've introduced legislation in the Senate to fund this promising avenue of research.

The Respect for Life Pluripotent Stem Cell Act of 2005 would have authorized $15 million for the National Institutes of Health to develop ethical techniques to create and study pluripotent stem cells. The bill would also have prohibited any research that would harm or destroy a human embryo while directing studies on animal models to develop and test techniques for producing human pluripotent stem cells.

Congress should pursue alternatives that offer all of the benefits of embryonic stem cell research without opening a Pandora's box of ethical problems. At the dawn of the biotech century, advocating taxpayer-funded destructive experimentation on human embryos that will be "thrown away anyway" would set us on a dangerous course. If human life is sacred and worthy of protection unless it is unwanted or destined for destruction, then many human lives, including those of the terminally ill or severely handicapped, would be cheapened and endangered.

The response many supporters of destructive embryonic stem cell research offer to these ethical concerns is troubling. Rather than offering a coherent ethical statement on when human life deserves protection, some of the more fervent supporters of research on embryonic stem cells prefer to portray critics as unscientific or even superstitious. This stance is ironic considering that more faith is required to believe in an avenue of research that has not produced any therapies than an avenue that has produced therapies.

The development of research on embryonic stem cells as an article of faith is evident in news coverage. When the *Washington Post* reported on the breakthrough at Harvard, its headline said the development would "muddle" the debate. When a scientist is able to set aside bias, any new factual discovery provides clarity, not confusion. A more ominous explanation for the lack of enthusiasm for the Harvard announcement is that researchers want to keep the door open to "fetal farming"–a process by which embryos are cloned, implanted, and harvested for spare organs. Studies on animals are showing that the real potential of research on embryonic stem cells is found in embryos that are not days old but weeks old, when tissue growth can be controlled.

The biotechnology industry understands that science is headed in this direction, which perhaps is one reason why the U.S. Senate is still to the left of the United Nations General Assembly on the question of human cloning. The United Nations has called for a complete cloning ban, and most European countries have already enacted such a ban.

The United States is not in danger of "falling behind" the rest of the world in embryonic stem cell research. What we are in danger of doing is falling behind the rest of the world when it comes to protecting the sanctity of life. America's greatest contribution to the world has not been our industry or science but our ideas. We have led the world in protecting the dignity of the individual, which has made all of our other achievements possible. We should not cast aside our core principles for a misguided bill that might yield temporary political gain but failed experiments and an ethical quandary for future generations.

This piece originally appeared in The Hill Newspaper, *and it has been modified only to reflect that some actions that were current are now in the past tense.*

THE PLEDGE OF ALLEGIANCE: SEPARATION OF CHURCH AND STATE

PROBABLY EVERY SCHOOL-AGED CHILD IN AMERICA IS asked to recite the Pledge of Allegiance each school day. Most people think, what's the big deal? It's only a short patriotic song that reinforces our common connection, namely, that we are Americans. For those who object, the big deal is religion. And religion has been a big deal since the inception of our country.

Religion was a sensitive subject for our forefathers. Religious organizations held significant influence over political matters in early American colonies. During this period, laws commonly regulated both moral and political life. For example, the Virginia colony's moral laws included a five-shilling fine for swearing and a ten-shilling fine for gambling. And in the political arena government officials were required to swear allegiance to a specific religion in order to hold office.

But as the colonies moved towards independence, these laws began to conflict with the emerging concept of individual liberty. This eventually led to cries for reform, which in turn laid the foundation for the separation of church and state. Religious freedom, along with the concept of separation that is enshrined in the First Amendment, is one of our country's founding principles. Thomas Jefferson and James Madison are credited with shaping the First Amendment (and the famous phrase "the wall between church and state" is specifically attributed to Jefferson). Under their influence the First Amendment was created in order to defend religious freedom in two distinct ways: by restricting the government's involvement with religion and by protecting the religious activity of individuals.

Jefferson's Perspective

When America was still young (1785), the Virginia legislature considered a bill that would have extended the collection of taxes to support the established church. Both Jefferson and Madison led the fight against this tax. They prevailed, and the legislature instead enacted Virginia's Act for Establishing Religious Freedom.

Jefferson's position does not mean that he was against religion. In fact, most, if not all, of the Founding Fathers believed in God. In the preamble to this bill, Jefferson's words provide insight into his view of God, religious liberty and the relationship between the two:

"Whereas Almighty God hath created the mind free; that all attempts to influence it by temporal punishments or burthens, or by civil incapacitations, tend only to beget habits of hypocrisy and meanness, and are a departure from the plan of the Holy author of our religion . . . that the impious presumption of legislators and rulers, civil as well as ecclesiastical, who being themselves but fallible and uninspired men, have assumed dominion over the faith of others, setting up their own opinions and modes of thinking as the only true and infallible, and as such endeavouring to impose them on others, hath established and maintained false religions over the greatest part of the world, and through all time . . . that our civil rights have no dependence

> on our religious opinions, any more than our opinions in physics or geometry."

Religion in the First Amendment

> "Congress shall make no law respecting an establishment of religion, or prohibiting the free exercise thereof."

Religion is specifically mentioned in two independent phrases. The first phrase is the Establishment Clause. Establishment limits the government's ability to *establish* or set up a state religion (although it has been interpreted to apply more broadly, as will be discussed). The second phrase is the Free Exercise Clause. Free Exercise addresses an individual's right to *exercise* or practice his/her religious beliefs. Together they form the Religion Clauses. This chapter deals only with the Establishment Clause portion.

Before we jump into the abyss, let's start with what we know. There are established principles restricting the type of laws that federal, state, and local governments may pass that impact religion or religious activity:

1. A government may not set up a church.

2. A government may not participate in religious organizations.
3. A government may not aid or favor one religion over another.
4. Generally, a government is restricted from giving money directly to religious organizations in order to support religious activities.
5. If a government does give out money to a religious institution, then it must do so for a non-religious purpose and without favoritism.

Those fundamentals are established. But now comes the complicated part.

You can't play the "the Constitution-says-this" game unless you are prepared to explain what should lie underneath broad statements such as, "the idea of a separation of church and state." In the First Amendment arena, that means tackling the issue of how government *should* interact with religion. Should government be totally excluded from religion to the point where no government resources go to religious organizations? Or should the government embrace religion by supporting programs that have religious elements? Here is the range of options that exist for defining "separation."

Separation of Church and State

1. Government and religion are totally separate.

The government cannot support or aid any religious activity whatsoever. Although total separation implies that the city fire department could not enter a burning church, mosque, or synagogue, the more practical idea is that there should be as much separation as realistically possible.

2. Government is neutral towards religion–no endorsement and no coercion.

The government is neutral but not completely separate from religion. The focus is how citizens perceive the government's role and its relationship to religion. For example, the government may fund religious activity provided it isn't either attempting to influence people to accept a religious belief or endorsing religion.

3. Government accommodates religion.

The government recognizes the role of religion in our country's heritage and openly supports it. A government can directly fund religious activity, provided it does not give preferential treatment to any one religion over the others.

You can see that there are vastly different ways to define separation. And how one feels about separation depends upon one's point of view on how the relationship between God and government should be defined. The Supreme Court is made up of nine Justices, each with his or her own constitutional view (not necessarily their personal view) on the church and state relationship. That's why it should not come as a surprise that these different philosophies come into play when the Court evaluates the constitutionality of a specific law.

Generally, the Court will measure a law against an established standard or test. Unfortunately, in this area there is no agreed-upon standard, and a big part of the Court's debate is over which test(s) to apply. As a result, the Court has bounced between three tests to evaluate whether or not governmental laws satisfy the Establishment Clause. The fact that none of these tests have won anything close to unanimous support should tell you that there is lively debate about how the Court should apply the broad principle of separation of church and state.

Three Tests: Lemon, Endorsement, and Coercion

1. Lemon Test

The Lemon test examines a law's purpose and effect. The government law or action must have a "secular (non-religious) purpose." The law's "primary effect" must neither benefit nor burden religion. Additionally, the effect cannot lead to "excessive entanglement" between government and religion (for example, requiring the government to monitor future activities).

2. Endorsement Test

The Endorsement test focuses on how an individual perceives government action. The law cannot cause a reasonable person to believe that the government is "endorsing" religion. One example is whether the law creates a division between insiders (people whose views are favored by the message) and outsiders (people whose views are at odds with the message). The law also must not excessively entangle government and religion.

3. The Coercion Test

The Coercion test also focuses on the individual's perspective. Here, the law cannot "coerce" or in any way force people to participate in religion against their will.

Like one's views on separation, the tests also represent different ways to interpret the broad concept of the relationship between church and state. Each test reflects a position of more or less tolerance towards religion. Using the Lemon test will generally lead to greater separation because the test looks at both the purpose and effect of the law. Quite simply, the test is harder to pass. By contrast, the Endorsement and Coercion tests are usually more accepting of government involvement in religion because the focus is on the perception of the observer.

To understand this difference more clearly, consider the example of a city's holiday display that hangs above the city hall. If the city council's purpose is to promote a religious sentiment, then the display probably will not pass the Lemon test, regardless of how it impacts observers. However, if observers only see the display as a harmless reminder of the season and do not interpret it as an endorsement of religion, then that same display might pass both the Endorsement and Coercion tests. Same display, different results.

If you find this utterly confusing, don't fret . . . it's confusing to a lot of folks. Hopefully this next example will help clear things up.

The Pledge of Allegiance

Now, please rise for . . . the Pledge of Allegiance.

"I pledge allegiance to the flag of the United States of America, and to the Republic for which it stands, one nation *under God*, indivisible, with liberty and justice for all."

Ah, yes, brings back happy memories of playing ball on the blacktop. You know, the good old days.

Anyway, a few years before any of us were in grade school, 1492 to be exact, Christopher Columbus discovered the place we now call home. Four hundred years later, the Pledge of Allegiance was written so that school children could commemorate Columbus's discovery. This original version did not contain any reference to God, and for sixty years the text of the Pledge remained virtually unchanged.

After World War II, the United States and the USSR entered into the Cold War, a war that was characterized by little direct combat and lots of political rhetoric. One fundamental aspect of the conflict was different religious ideologies: God-fearing American values opposed to those of the God-less Communists. As a way to distinguish our beliefs, the U.S. Congress added two words–"under God"–to the Pledge of Allegiance. This sentiment was reinforced several years later when the phrase "In God We Trust" was adopted as our nation's official slogan, and then placed on U.S. dollar bills. (It has been on U.S. coins since 1864.)

Today, students all across the country regularly start their day by reciting the Pledge. This practice satisfies the legal requirement of states such as California that each school day begin with an appropriate patriotic exercise.

Requiring Students to Recite the Pledge Is Unconstitutional

The issue of whether a school could require students to recite the original Pledge (before the "under God" language was added) was decided in 1943 by the U.S. Supreme Court (West Virginia State Board of Education v. Barnette). The State of West Virginia made the flag salute mandatory, meaning that a child could not passively watch but was required to participate by raising his/her hand. Violations of this law had stiff penalties; a child could be punished with expulsion and placement in a juvenile reformatory, while his parents faced a fifty-dollar fine and thirty days in prison.

Barnette was a member of the Jehovah's Witnesses, a group that refused to salute the flag because it conflicted with their religious beliefs. According to the Book of Exodus (Chapter 20), "Thou shalt not make . . . any graven image," and the Witnesses considered the flag an image.

The Court determined that a government could neither compel nor suppress speech, because to do so would give government an unacceptable degree of control over the free minds and spirits of individuals. In one of the most eloquent and often quoted statements, the Court said:

"If there is any fixed star in our constitutional constellation, it is that no official, high or petty, can prescribe what shall be orthodox in politics, nationalism, religion, or other matters of opinion, or force citizens to confess by word or act their faith therein."

And that brings us to the most recent Pledge case.

Michael Newdow's Daughter

Dr. Michael Newdow is an atheist whose daughter was enrolled in a California public elementary school in 2000. As part of the school's morning regimen, the students in his daughter's class recited the Pledge of

Allegiance. Newdow objected to this practice because he believed it put his daughter in a no-win situation–she either had to recite the Pledge and recognize the existence of God, or be singled out as the lone student who refused to participate. Newdow believed that under these circumstances his daughter had no meaningful choice, and that the State–through its State-run school with State-paid employees–was forcing his daughter to adopt its view that God exists. In other words, the government was establishing a religious preference in favor of God. Since the Pledge was religion-free at its inception, he argued that Congress's addition of the phrase "under God" to the Pledge violated the Establishment Clause.

That case (Newdow v. Elk Grove Unified School District, 2004) garnered significant media attention. Although the case made it to the U.S. Supreme Court (but was dismissed for other, non-religious reasons), the question of whether the Pledge violated the Establishment Clause was ultimately decided by the Ninth Circuit Court of Appeals. In examining the case, the Ninth Circuit applied all three tests–Lemon, Endorsement, and Coercion–to determine whether reciting the Pledge in school violated the Constitution. The court found that because of the "under God" language, the Pledge failed all three tests. Here's their reasoning:

The Lemon Test:
The first part of the Lemon test requires that the law have a non-religious purpose. The stated purpose in adding the language was to encourage students to swear allegiance to our nation and to God. This is clear from President Eisenhower's comments the day he signed the law that added "under God" to the Pledge:

" . . . millions of our school children will daily proclaim . . . the dedication of our nation and our people to the Almighty."

Because "under God" was specifically added in order to promote a religious belief in the Almighty, the law appears to have a religious purpose and fails Lemon.

Endorsement Test:
The Endorsement test prohibits the State from endorsing a religious belief. When a person recites the Pledge, they are literally pledging their allegiance to the values that are represented by the flag: liberty, justice, and the belief that we are a nation under God.

Here, the words "under God" promote a religious belief, namely, the belief in *one* God.

The State's endorsement of monotheism is equivalent to stating that we are a nation under Zeus, Buddha, or under no God at all, because under any of these statements the State is taking a stance on religion. This creates a division between "insiders," those who see the government's position as supporting their belief in God, and "outsiders," people who feel the government's position is at odds with their beliefs. Because the "under God" version of the Pledge creates a perception that the State of California is endorsing religion–either in general or one particular brand of religion–it fails the Endorsement test.

Coercion Test:

The Coercion test prohibits the State from coercing people to adopt a religious belief. When the State leads students in reciting a religiously based message, it fails to remain neutral. Here, the State is forcing students to profess a particular religious belief. School-age students are very impressionable, and peer pressure influences them to act the same way and follow the same rules as other students and teachers. Although technically they can choose not to participate, given their age and the social expectation, it would extremely difficult for them to make that choice. By putting young children in this unfair, no-win position, the State is coercing students into participating in a religious activity. Thus, it fails the Coercion test.

In order to further emphasize its position, the Ninth Circuit pointed out that the phrase "under God" could not be interpreted as merely a description of the fact that many Americans believe in God. Since, in the court's opinion, the phrase had religious connotations, its use in the Pledge violated the principle that government must remain neutral towards religion. And this contradicted the idea of religious freedom that is expressed in the Establishment Clause.

The Counter Argument–The Pledge IS Constitutional

As often happens in our system, intelligent minds can differ. In this case, a sister court of the Ninth Circuit–the Seventh Circuit–considered exactly the same issue and concluded differently. In Sherman v. Community Consolidated School District (1992), the Seventh Circuit looked at an Illinois law that required students in public schools to recite the Pledge.

In support of its conclusion that the Pledge was constitutional, the court addressed the religious aspect of the Pledge head on. It attempted to distinguish between religious statements and what it called "ceremonial references" to God that could be found in presidential speeches, the Declaration of Independence, and the *Star Spangled Banner.*

What's a "Ceremonial Reference"?

The phrase "ceremonial reference" refers to the idea that there are religious words or symbols that, over time, have taken on more of a cultural than religious meaning. One prominent example of a ceremonial reference is the words "In God We Trust" on our currency. Arguably they have become so much a part of our civic life that the phrase cannot be interpreted as a governmental attempt to promote a religious belief.

In looking at this issue, the Seventh Circuit found that the reference to God in the Pledge could be understood in this ceremonial or cultural sense. For example, "under God" could be understood as a simple recognition of the fact that our forefathers believed in God. It could also mean that a belief in God is part of our cultural heritage. The ceremonial reference to God in the Pledge is consistent with our nation's long tradition of references to God in historical speeches and documents and even the words used to open the court: "God save the United States and this honorable Court." So by using this phrase, the Pledge–and therefore the government–is not making a statement about or taking a particular position on religion.

As for the tests, the Seventh Circuit pointed to the Supreme Court's uncertainty in this area of law (and the fact that under the Court's previous rulings, no one test was established as *the* test to apply). Given the lack of a clear standard to use, the Seventh Circuit felt free to choose how to interpret the law. Thus, it did not apply any of the tests used by the Ninth Circuit, and it came up with a different result.

Conclusion

That's where we stand today. The Court, at some point in time, will likely consider whether the Pledge violates the Constitution. More critically, the wall between church and state could slide as the make-up of the Court changes (and, with it, the judicial philosophies of new Justices). Until the next case, have fun arguing with your friends and family on that subject. And if you are walking in your town's civic center, pay closer attention to any holiday displays. Consider whether you think the government is promoting a general religious message, one particular brand of religion, or no religious message at all.

ESSAY

Hon. Kenneth Starr

Former Independent Counsel

The Founding of the American Republic represented an enormous step forward in the science and art of government. First and foremost, the theory of the Founding, embodied in the Declaration of Independence, was that individual rights were derived from higher, non-earthly authority. Government was ordained to secure rights irrevocably conferred by the Creator. That theistic-rich theory of rights–and their origin–was then given further, more concrete expression in the First Amendment. There, in the opening sixteen words of the first enumeration of rights under the Bill of Rights, the philosophy of the Declaration was reaffirmed. Congress was to make no law abridging the pre-existing, primordial set of rights that included–as the first of the first freedoms–religious liberty. Tellingly, the Founding generation agreeably embraced a definition of religion as "the duty that [an individual] owes to the Creator."

Second, this theologically rich, foundational theory of rights has never been abandoned or jettisoned over the course of our unfolding history as the oldest republic on the face of the earth. In all amendments, whether ratified or merely proposed, and in the occasional calls for a constitutional convention over the course of the nation's history, not once has a serious call been made to reexamine the philosophical basis of individual rights articulated at the time of the Declaration. To the contrary, one of the few holidays that truly unites Divided America to this day is the Fourth of July, where we celebrate our birth as a nation and take note of Jefferson's immortal expression of the worldview that justified our bloody rebellion.

Third, this time-honored, well-settled theory of human rights itself reflected a magnificent step in shaping attitudes toward the intellectual and moral basis of human liberty. John Locke and other great theorists of human liberty unabashedly summoned forth supra-human authority as the basis for liberal notions of freedom of conscience. These notions were heartily embraced by a young republic that, at every turn, lifted up the value of faith communities–and of religion more generally–as at minimum helpful and perhaps even indispensable in securing ordered liberty.

It was therefore entirely natural for the first Congress–the very Congress that fashioned the venerated words of the First Amendment–also to engage (at taxpayer expense) a member of the clergy to serve as a chaplain and to begin legislative sessions with prayer. The pivotal message of the First Amendment was, in short, prevention of official recognition of a church or violations of freedom of conscience. It was emphatically not to eradicate all references to God or religion more generally from our official life. So it has been that, without interruption, Congress, whether controlled by Democrats or Republicans, has always had a paid chaplain who begins each session with an invocation of the blessing of God.

This simple example of uninterrupted practice vividly demonstrates that the effort to excise references of "under God" from the Pledge of Allegiance represents a complete departure from our constitutional traditions. If change is to come, and the two challenged words purged from the Pledge, that change should come only from the process of thoughtful deliberation through the political process. It is through that process that we identify, and change, who and what we are as a people. The post-Civil War Amendments bear witness to the democratic ideal that epic change should come through the will of the people through their representative institutions. Those convulsive changes manifestly should not come from judicial interpretation of words that simply will not bear the meaning that Pledge opponents seek to champion. The short answer to the challengers of the words "under God," is to direct their grievances to the American people and their representatives.

So what does the First Amendment's protection of religious liberty, properly interpreted, mean? At bottom, it means that Americans are to enjoy the fullest possible extent and range of protections for religious activity and religious expression. It means that the government is to be wary of interfering with faith communities, or taking sides in the clash of religious ideas or theologies. It further means, as it did of old, that freedom of conscience should be honored. No one should be forced to say the Pledge, or to utter the particular words that give rise to an offense to conscience.

This then was the Great Philosophical Compromise of the Founding: The nation could in fact, and necessarily did, have an animating vision and worldview that justified the revolution and the establishment of a new political order. The Compromise also meant that not all persons had to assent to that animating worldview. Freedom should ring, including at a decidedly individual level. A non-believer could, without fear of governmental interference, decry Jefferson's lofty sentiments as mere claptrap. So too, the non-believer could, and still can, say that "I will not utter words with which I profoundly disagree." The proper constitutional response is, "more power to you." This is a free country, and coercion of belief and matters of conscience will simply not be allowed. The non-believer, in short, is to enjoy the same full measure of freedom of thought–or what Justice Robert Jackson eloquently called the freedom of the mind–as all other members of the polity.

What the non-believer cannot successfully do is to tear down the intellectual and historical underpinning of our rights as individuals through judicial interpretation of words meant to ensure the maximum of religious liberty. To the contrary, our history can–and I believe should–be honored in non-coercive ways. To embrace the national motto, "In God We Trust," is to recognize our history and tradition, uttered by every President–including Madison and Jefferson–and given immortal voice by Abraham Lincoln at Gettysburg when he drew from our cultural traditions, looked back at the Declaration and the Revolution, and called for a new birth of freedom for this nation "under God."

Thus, what Congress did in 1954 was to more fully state the philosophical basis of the American experiment, as given voice by Lincoln in the throes of the terrible Civil War. Something was missing. Ours was not simply "one nation." That could be said of Canada, or France, or Mexico. No, our Founding was distinctive and particularistic. It was a nation founded "under God," as evidenced by the words of the Declaration itself, the embrace of Declaration values in the First Amendment, and Lincoln's eloquent expression on a cold battlefield in 1863. This is likely to endure as long as the Republic itself stands, and should stand until we embark on a new philosophical course that would justify the case for human liberty and freedom of conscience.

PHYSICIAN-ASSISTED SUICIDE

THE CONSTITUTION PROTECTS "LIFE" AND "LIBERTY," which at the very least means that no one has the right to take your life–except, of course, when the government sentences you to death. But how broadly should the right to life be interpreted? Should it mean that one has total control over one's life? And, if so, would that include the choice to end one's own life? From a public policy perspective, do we want to empower individuals to make life-ending decisions, usually in the midst of a terminal illness or other personal crisis? And, equally troubling, do we want to allow other people to represent us in making that decision?

Once again, we are faced with a fundamental rights question. The Fourteenth Amendment to the Constitution recognizes the right to "life," but what other rights can be implied from that one? Obviously this is a challenging question, the answer to which raises a range of moral and ethical issues. Here is the Supreme Court case that first addressed some of these issues.

The Case of Nancy Cruzan

In 1983, twenty-five-year-old Nancy Cruzan was in a near-fatal car accident. She was found lying face down in a ditch and was not breathing. She was transported to the hospital, where she was diagnosed with severe brain bruises. Permanent brain damage usually results after six minutes without oxygen to the brain. It was estimated that Nancy Cruzan's brain lacked oxygen for twelve to fourteen minutes. After three weeks in a coma, Nancy moved into an unconscious state. In that condition, she displayed basic motor reflexes but exhibited no significant brain functions. Despite all efforts to rehabilitate her further, Nancy's condition never improved. From the time of her accident in 1983 until her death in 1990, Nancy Cruzan lived in a Missouri hospital on life support and in a vegetative state.

After it appeared that Nancy was not likely to emerge from her vegetative state her parents asked the hospital to remove her from life support. Because the hospital refused to honor Nancy's parents' request without a court order, their request made it all the way to the United States Supreme Court. In Cruzan v. Missouri Health Department, (1990), the Court was asked to determine whether the Constitution protects the fundamental right to die.

Is the Right to Die a Fundamental Right Protected by the Constitution?

We touched on the importance of fundamental rights in an earlier chapter. The critical issue to remember in this regard is that the Constitution specifically mentions some rights, while others are implied. The difficulty arises in deciding where to draw the line as one right is implied from another (or possibly a third). If you haven't read that part of the book yet, or want a refresher, here's another analogy.

You've seen the style of painting where a picture is made up of lots of dots (it's called pointillism). In the middle of the painting there are thousands of dots, but as you look toward the edges you see fewer and fewer. If you were asked to circle *only* the dots that make up "the picture," you would have to decide which dots to include. You could make a big circle that included every single dot on the canvas, but that would probably include random dots that are not critical to the picture. On the other hand, you could make a tight circle around only the dots that are primary focus of the picture, but that might leave out some dots that are still important. The process of deciding where to draw the boundary around "the picture" is similar to distinguishing between fundamental and non-fundamental rights (and, don't forget, as a judge you then have to justify why one dot is part of the picture but another dot, that happens to be very close by, is not part of the picture).

In Nancy's case, the Court was required to evaluate two questions: First, since the Constitution protects "life" and "liberty," should this be interpreted to also include a fundamental right to refuse medical treatment; and second, if so, how should the Court balance that right against the State of Missouri's equally valid interest in preserving life?

A Constitutional Right to Refuse Medical Treatment

Here's the argument that the Constitution protects the right to refuse medical treatment: The abortion cases illustrated that the Constitution protects an individual's right to bodily privacy and autonomy. This means you, and only you, control what goes on with your body. And if you are forced to accept medical treatment that you did not want, then someone else is exercising control over your body. Since that situation conflicts with bodily autonomy, the Constitution must also protect your right to refuse treatment. As a result, you have the right to terminate your life support even if that action will cause your death. Furthermore, if you have left proper instructions, then someone else is empowered to instruct the hospital to do the same. In other words, you (or someone you identify) can refuse medical treatment by stopping life support, even if that brings about your death. The right to refuse medical treatment is a protected right.

Once the Court recognized Nancy's fundamental right to reject medical treatment, the next issue to consider was how to balance that right with the State's equally valid interest in protecting life. Missouri State law provided that it was okay to withdraw life support if it could be shown that this was–or would have been–Nancy's intent when she was conscious. The standard of proof required to establish Nancy's wishes was "clear and convincing" evidence.

Levels of Proof

Beyond a reasonable doubt–the highest level of proof, and the required standard in all criminal cases. The evidence must establish that there is no doubt "that prevents one from being firmly convinced" that a person is guilty.

Clear and convincing–a middle level of proof, which is used when lawmakers decide that what's at stake warrants a higher standard than simply preponderance. It means that it is "highly probable" or "reasonably certain" that something happened, and that this degree of certainty is supported by "clear and convincing" evidence.

Preponderance–the lowest level of proof, and the standard for civil cases. It means that based on the evidence it is more likely than not–just over 50 percent–that the person is responsible for some civil action.

The State of Missouri required "clear and convincing" as the level of proof because it had anticipated that there might be times when a dying person's intentions are unclear because the patient is unable to communicate her wishes. Given what's at stake, and the ability of a third party to make this decision, the State required a higher legal standard.

Recognizing the same concern, the Supreme Court points out, "there will be unfortunate instances in which the family members will not act in the patient's best interests." As a result, it upheld the Missouri standard that required clear and convincing evidence because it determined that the Missouri law did not unreasonably infringe her right. In other words, they struck a balance between Nancy's fundamental right and the State's interest in preserving life. (Although Nancy's parents did not have clear and convincing evidence of Nancy's desires at the time of the case, they were later able to produce additional evidence, and the State allowed Nancy's life support to be terminated.)

But Cruzan only addressed the first part of the physician-assisted suicide issue. Remember, the Court decided whether Nancy had a right to refuse treatment . . . which leads us to the next question. Is the right to *refuse* treatment to save one's life the same as the right to *receive* treatment to end one's life?

Life Saving vs. Life Ending Treatment

Although the right to refuse treatment is constitutionally protected, the question of whether the Constitution protects a person's right to obtain assistance to end one's life had yet to be decided when the Court heard Cruzan's case. But physician-assisted suicide was the issue in Washington v. Glucksburg (1997), where several Washington doctors challenged a Washington State law that made it a crime to assist another person in ending his life. In that case, the doctors claimed that the Constitution protected the "right to die." The State of Washington countered that the Constitution did not recognize "the right to commit suicide." And so, once again, the Court had to decide whether a right is fundamental (based on whether or not it can be implied from another fundamental right).

The Doctors' Argument

The doctors offered two arguments in support of the idea that the Constitution protects the right to physician-assisted suicide: First, the right to die can be inferred from the right to choose to have an abortion. If the right to *control* your body means anything, then it must allow a person to make the ultimate choice–whether or not to keep your body alive. Second, the right to die can also be inferred from the right to refuse medical treatment. The doctors argued that Nancy's case was not simply about refusing medical treatment; it was about the bigger issue of Nancy's right to die in the manner she desired. Under either argument the Court should recognize a fundamental right to physician-assisted suicide.

The Court's Perspective

The Court, however, didn't agree with either of these arguments. In its view, this case was neither about the right to die nor the right to control the way you die. Rather, the issue in Glucksburg was whether the Constitution recognized a fundamental right to commit suicide. And in the Court's view, the right to commit suicide could not be implied through either the right to bodily autonomy (so, out goes the first argument that it's akin to abortion) or the right to refuse medical treatment (so, out goes the second argument that it's like Nancy's situation).

The Court explained the difference between *refusing* and *receiving* treatment by comparing the goals of patients in these two situations. It reasoned that in refusing medical treatment, a patient's goal is to be free of the intrusion of tubes, tests, and other invasive procedures. Such patients are managing the quality of their lives and are not actively trying to bring about their death. In addition, the Court explained that what ultimately kills a patient who refuses medical treatment is the underlying disease that is the source of their illness. Not accepting treatment simply allows a natural process to continue. In contrast, a patient who requests assistance in dying is actively ending his life. It's the difference between dying naturally and committing suicide. By viewing the issue in this light, the Court felt that protecting a right to physician-assisted suicide would be like condoning murder.

In arriving at this position the Court examined the long and consistent treatment of suicide over hundreds of years. The overwhelming consensus in the legal traditions of civilized nations had always been against suicide. Suicide is just like murder, the only difference is that the victim is oneself. Consequently, the Court upheld the Washington law prohibiting physician-assisted suicide. The right to commit suicide is not a fundamental right protected by the Constitution.

In 1994, voters in the State of Oregon passed the Death with Dignity Act. The Act allows "terminally-ill Oregonians to end their lives through the voluntary self-administration of lethal medications, expressly prescribed by a physician for that purpose." In order to qualify, a patient must be: (1) At least eighteen years old; (2) an Oregon resident; (3) capable of making health care decisions for him/her self; and (4) suffering from a terminal illness that will result in death within six months.

In a case that made it up to the U.S. Supreme Court (Gonzales v. State of Oregon, 2005), the Death with Dignity Act was found to fall within the rights of the State of Oregon, since the federal government has no authority to prevent Oregon from providing lethal medications to willing and mentally competent people.

An Afterthought

Although the entire Court agreed with the outcome of this case, four of the Justices suggested that they might have found a constitutional right in a slightly different circumstance. These Justices explained that there is no reason why someone in pain should be made to suffer, and that the "right to die in order to avoid pain" might receive constitutional protection. But that was not the case here, and such a case has yet to make it in front of the Court.

Cruzan and Glucksburg were decided over ten years ago. Even if someone heard of them at the time, they have long been forgotten for most people. The more recent example of this issue is that of Terri Schindler-Schiavo.

Terri Schindler-Schiavo: A Tragic Example of Constitutional Structure

Many people are familiar with the tragic events surrounding the death of Terri Schindler-Schiavo, the young Florida woman whose family and husband fought a bitter battle over removal of her life support. In a sense, this was the worst scenario playing out in reality. A family pulled apart, each with different views of the facts and of what Terri might have wanted. Numerous legal challenges eventually led to a final court order allowing the removal of Terri's feeding and hydration tubes.

One of these legal challenges was in response to a law passed by the Florida State legislature. The law granted the Governor of Florida the authority to prevent someone in Terri's condition from being denied food and water (helping Terri appeared to be the legislature's specific purpose, as the Governor's authority under the law was to expire fifteen days after the law was passed). The Florida Supreme Court reviewed whether the law was valid under the Florida constitution and determined that the law violated the concept of separation of powers.

The United States Constitution has a very simple structure: three independent branches, each with its own base of power and authority. As we all remember from grade school, the legislature (Congress) makes the rules, the executive (the President) carries them out, and the judiciary (the court system) has the final say about what all three branches can (and cannot) do. This structure is known as the separation of powers, and it ensures that one branch does not intrude on the rights of another. By dividing the tasks of running a democracy, separation of powers keeps each branch's decisions within a well-defined zone of power.

But separation of powers is only half the beauty of the Constitution. I'm sure you remember the other half . . . checks and balances. Checks and balances is a further safeguard that is built into our three-part system. It provides a way for the branches to influence decisions made by the other branches. For example, although the power to make laws is given to Congress, the President has the ability to veto these laws. The ability of the President to veto a law acts as a check on Congress's power.

The power to check also works the other way. Although the President picks the members of his cabinet, Congress has the right to approve (and impeach) them. Checks and balances also affect the judicial branch. Although courts have the last say about a particular case, the President nominates and Congress confirms and can impeach all judicial appointees. Furthermore, if Congress and the President do not agree with the Court, then they can either pass a new law or attempt to amend the Constitution. Finally, certain powers are split between branches. For example, the President and Congress both share the power to enter into war. Congress has the ability to declare war but the President, as the Commander-in-Chief, can defend the nation without congressional approval. In other words, the power to put the nation at war is shared.

Back to Terri. According to the Florida Supreme Court, the decision about whether to remove Terri Schindler-Schiavo's nutrition and hydration tubes had been made by Florida courts. When the Florida legislature passed a law giving the Governor special authority, the legislature was attempting to get around the court's decision. The court called this "an invasion of the authority of the judicial branch." Why? Because, as we just discussed, the constitution (in this case, of the State of Florida) gives the judiciary the power to make the final decision in cases before the court. And under separation of powers, the court's decision is "not reviewable by the Governor." In other words, although the Florida State legislature has the authority to pass laws, it does not have the power to authorize the Governor of Florida to overturn decisions of the Florida courts.

Conclusion

On a practical level, physician-assisted suicide is an example of how the law must address the most difficult issues and balance the most divided interests. This includes the standards required by a State in order to enforce a request to end one's life and which individual is empowered to present that decision on a patient's behalf.

On a moral level, this issue raises even more challenging questions (for some, although not for all). If the patient expresses a clear desire to end his life, shouldn't we honor that request rather than requiring him to stay alive and suffer? On the other hand, aren't we condoning death and devaluing life by even providing this option?

Finally, what should one make of the State of Oregon's role in (arguably) facilitating death? Merciful? Atrocious?

ESSAY

Bobby Schindler

Terri Schindler-Schiavo's Brother

On March 31, 2005, my sister, Terri Schindler-Schiavo, died of dehydration. Her feeding tube was removed by court order on the hearsay testimony of her guardian, Michael Schiavo. My sister lived in a neurologically compromised state for reasons that are still unknown. My family wanted nothing from anyone but to be granted the permission to care for Terri for the span of her natural life. We were denied. Terri tenaciously fought for more than thirteen days after being deprived of the most basic, natural, and constant need that we all share: the need for nourishment–food and water. Contrary to the reports in the media, this was not an "end-of-life" issue. Terri was not on a respirator, not terminally ill, not dying, and not succumbing to any killer disease. She was disabled. She was dependent on others. But she was still very much a life, a woman, and a person.

It has become quite obvious to my family that the mainstream media played a critical role in society accepting the rationalizations offered to justify killing Terri (and other disabled individuals in similar situations). The popular media has and continues to report the circumstances of Terri's case incorrectly and omit key information, and they have consistently acted without objectivity. Here are a few examples.

The media did not miss an opportunity to report the pro-life community's support for Terri. What they conveniently left out was the more than twenty-five local and national disability organizations standing shoulder to shoulder with my family. It seems that selective reporting provided an easier way to portray Terri's situation, ignoring the truth that she was an innocent disabled woman being starved and dehydrated to death. The media's coverage of the involvement of Congress in helping Terri is another example. The media never properly explained what Congress did, which was to provide Terri a federal review–required for those on death row just before execution. Additionally, the fact that Judge Greer violated Florida law by acting both as Terri's attorney and as judge in her case was not mentioned. Could you imagine the public outcry if the judge in a death penalty case also acted as the inmate's attorney? Instead, the media took issue with Congress interfering in a "private family matter," failing also to mention that this so-called private family matter involved Michael Schiavo himself hiring a lawyer to ask a judge to have his brain-injured wife put to death. The media questioned the idea that when a judge says an innocent woman should be killed, it is okay, but when Congress takes issue with such a matter it is abhorrent.

However, the most egregious error is the misreporting of Terri's autopsy. The media inexplicably continues to report that Terri was brain-dead. There is not one doctor on record as having diagnosed Terri with this condition. Furthermore, the medical examiner was unable to conclude whether Terri was even in a persistent vegetative state (PVS), because PVS is a clinical diagnosis and cannot be confirmed by autopsy. In addition, the consulting neuropathologist indicated that he could not rule out the possibility that Terri could have been in a minimally conscious state, a higher level of consciousness than would have been the case with the PVS diagnosis. Finally, Terri's frontal and temporal lobes, temporal poles, and insular cortex were relatively well-preserved, meaning that her brain was more normal in the areas that control higher-level thinking. All these critical facts, which support Terri's need for care and observation rather than justifying her death, were deliberately omitted from the media coverage. The few members of the media that had the integrity to speak the truth were drowned out by the many that perpetuated their own version of these events.

It seems to me that the media is going to great lengths to justify what Michael Schiavo did to my sister based on this type of erroneous reporting, and in doing so, advances this growing "quality-of-life" mentality that has gripped our nation. I believe that the prevalence of this perspective on the value of life, or lack thereof, is the greatest tragedy resulting from my sister's death.

Throughout the entire history of mankind, food and water has never been considered "medical care." Has society reached the inhumane place where we put convenience and "quality of life" on a pedestal above basic needs? Our nation now claims that the most basic human necessities–food and water–are "medical treatment" in order to justify killing those "unworthy of life." And for what? Primarily for economic reasons. And persons like my sister, with injuries and disabilities, are too often seen as not being worthy of life, not worth the investment.

It is beyond comprehension that we are seeing a culture of death impose its will upon society's weakest and most vulnerable members. Thomas Jefferson wrote in the Declaration of Independence: "We hold these truths to be self-evident, that all men are created equal and that they are endowed by their Creator with certain inalienable rights, among which are Life, Liberty, and the Pursuit of Happiness." This is the philosophy of our country, one that I and many others interpret to mean that no person or agency has the authority to pronounce another human being as "unworthy of life."

If you took away access to food and water from a dog, you would go to jail, and rightly so. Take away the same sustenance from my sister, and they call it "medical ethics." Sadly, it seems that our nation is accepting more easily every day the decisions that bioethicists, doctors, hospitals, the growing number of so-called ethics committees, or even "loved ones" can make regarding whether or not another human being should live or die based on this "quality-of-life" standard. There is no doubt that there are sacrifices to make–dedicating the time, money, and resources to take care of people that need the attention and love of a baby–but what other choice do we have?

Are we going to respect, care for, and love each other, in spite of disability, cost, or inconvenience, or are we going to resent one another based on those limitations, set a price limit on what it takes to care for one another, and continue to pass legislation that makes killing our disabled reminiscent of the euthanasia agenda that existed prior to the Holocaust? Simply put, are we going care for the disabled or we are going to kill them?

What has happened to our nation when our laws go much further to protect those on death row than they do to protect the disabled, the weakest among us? When parents have to literally beg to be allowed to care for their children? And when judges and doctors are granted the legal authority to subjectively sentence to death, in the most dehumanizing and barbaric way, those very people that need our love and compassion the most?

GUN CONTROL

TWENTY-SEVEN WORDS. THAT'S THE FULL TEXT OF THE Second Amendment to the Constitution. It reads:

> "A well regulated Militia, being necessary to the security of a free State, the right of the people to keep and bear arms, shall not be infringed."

For many years, this one sentence has been a constant source of national debate. Why? Because it's not at all clear what it means.

Here's the problem: The U.S. Constitution grants rights (or powers) to three groups: the federal government (e.g., the power to tax); the states (e.g., the power to police its citizens); and the people (e.g., the right to free speech). The rights mentioned in the

Second Amendment do not pertain to the federal government. So, the question is, does the right to keep and bear arms apply directly to the people (to an individual) or to the states? How you answer this question ultimately determines whether or not you believe in an individual's right to own a gun.

Historical Note

It is helpful to be reminded of the historical context in which the Constitution was written. You'll of course remember that a number of the states did not like the idea of a powerful national government. The states had just fought off the English. Fresh from the battlefield, the idea of giving up their rights to another political body who could control them was difficult to swallow. That concern is why the Constitution balances the decision-making authority between the federal government and the states *and* guarantees certain rights to individuals. One more thing: When the Constitution refers to the "State" and "the people," it means exactly what it says, the State (of California) and you, me, and Joe Citizen. So, who is the "Militia"?

The Constitution commands that states are

required to train and maintain a militia to "uphold the laws of the Union, suppress Insurrections and repel Invasions." In those days, the militia–men between the ages of sixteen and sixty–took the place of a national army. The Founding Fathers intentionally gave the states the right to have a militia, as opposed to creating a federal army, as a way for the people to protect their state against the federal government. But over time the militia was replaced by city, state, and federal law enforcement, and today the only militia recognized by the federal courts are the U.S. National Guard and the Naval Militia.

Most instances of constitutional interpretation involve consideration of at least two perspectives. In the case of the Second Amendment, it is not immediately clear which entity–the state or the individual–is being granted the right. Let's take a look at both positions.

Position One: It's the State's Right

This position holds that the right to keep and bear arms is given to the states, or to the people collectively as members of a state. This right is granted to the states for the purpose of protecting and *serving the State* as members of an armed militia. In other words, an individual is granted the right to carry a gun *only if* he is serving the state as a member of the militia.

Consequently, there is no individual right to keep and bear arms given directly to the people. Sorry, but James (Madison), Alexander (Hamilton), and the rest of the Founding Fathers just didn't trust you with that musket!

Position Two: It's My (Individual) Right

This position maintains that the right to keep and bear arms is given directly to the *people* in order to protect *both* the people's interests and the state's. Supporters of this position agree that one component of protecting the people's interests is to defend the state against invasion, but they contend that the right *also extends to* protecting personal interests such as property or family. Consequently, the right to bear arms is given directly to the people and not to the states.

So Whose Right Is It?

There are persuasive arguments on both sides. One way to see the differences is to recognize that you can get the answer you want by simply emphasizing one part of the Amendment.

> "A well regulated Militia, being necessary to the security of a free State, the right of the people to keep and bear arms, shall not be infringed."

If you focus on the beginning two phrases–"A well regulated Militia, being necessary to the security of a free State"–you can interpret the Amendment as talking about militias and the importance they play within the states. Based on that, you can minimize the people's rights and make the focus of the Amendment on militias and the states. Under this interpretation, the next phrase *should* have been written as; "the right of the people (of a state) to keep and bear arms." So, it's the state's right.

If you focus on the last two phrases–"the right of the people to keep and bear arms, shall not be infringed"–you can interpret the Amendment's reference to militia and the states as simply setting up the important part of the Amendment, namely, the right of the people. No need to revise the language; just ignore the preamble. It's the people's right, plain and simple.

Is one interpretation of the Amendment wrong or more right than the other? (See below for how courts go about interpreting the Constitution).

What the Supreme Court Says

The U.S. Supreme Court has the last word on the law. When the Court decides a case, it's "holding" either references only the specific facts of that case (in this specific circumstance, Joe did a, b, and c, so he is guilty of burglary), or creates a general rule (from now on, when anyone does a, b, and c, they are guilty of burglary).

When the Court limits its ruling to the specific facts of a particular case, its decision does not create a general rule for all the other courts to follow (because other cases will be different–different people, different setting, etc.). Consequently, lower courts are allowed to interpret the same issue according to how they see the law. In fact, conflicting interpretations of the same law frequently exist in the lower courts (as we saw in the case of the Pledge of Allegiance). One of the primary functions of the Supreme Court is to select cases that create opportunities to establish a uniform rule for all courts to follow.

Since the adoption of the Second Amendment in 1791, the U.S. Supreme Court has taken only one case that addressed whether the Constitution recognizes an individual's right to bear arms. Here's what it said.

Hierarchy of the Federal Judicial System:

- United States Supreme Court
- 13 Federal Circuit Courts of Appeals (Circuit Courts 1–12 & District of Columbia)
- 91 Federal District Courts (State Supreme Court decisions are also appealed to the U.S. Supreme Court.)

United States v. Miller: The Supreme Court Case

In United States v. Miller (1939), Mr. Miller was caught transporting a sawed-off shotgun across state lines in violation of the National Firearms Act (the 1939 version of congressional legislation regulating guns). He claimed that the Act violated his Second Amendment right to carry the weapon. The Supreme Court interpreted the Second Amendment as applying to the militia and states' rights and *not* to Mr. Miller (as an individual). Consequently, the Court concluded that the Second Amendment only grants an individual the right to carry a weapon when they are serving in a state militia.

For twelve Circuit Courts, the Miller decision settled the issue.

United States v. Miller: Twelve Circuit Courts' Interpretation

The courts that support or follow Miller all have one thing in common: They all argue (and some don't even argue, they simply state it as a fact) that Miller is the law. This means that, according to these courts, individuals do not have a constitutional right to own a gun except in relation to serving in the militia. Although the precise legal theories differ, the result in all these cases is the same: "Second Amendment . . . offers no protection for the individual's right to bear arms" (Ninth Circuit); "the individual's possession of arms is not related to the preservation or efficiency of a militia" (Eighth Circuit); "this court on several occasions emphasized that the Second Amendment furnishes no absolute right to firearms" (Third Circuit): "[Defendant] concludes that every citizen has the absolute right to keep arms. This broad conclusion has long been rejected." (Tenth Circuit).

However, one Circuit Court saw the issue differently. Here's the alternative interpretation of the same Supreme Court ruling.

United States v. Miller: An Alternative Interpretation

In United States v. Emerson (2001), the Fifth Circuit Court of Appeals took a different position on Miller. Its interpretation? The case was only decided on Miller's specific situation, and the decision did not address the broader issue of whether the Second Amendment grants the right to individuals to bear arms. The court claims that Miller lost his case and was denied his individual right to bear arms simply because he had the wrong gun.

Here's the Fifth Circuit's reasoning: The Second Amendment grants the right to bear arms when an individual serves in the militia. And when you serve, you have to have a gun that is suitable for service. But Mr. Miller had a sawed-off shotgun, which is not suitable for serving in the militia. Because he had the "wrong" gun, his gun ownership can't possibly be connected to serving in the militia. So, of course, the Supreme Court did not find that the Second Amendment protected Miller's individual right to bear arms.

Put another way, the Fifth Circuit claimed that the Miller decision only addressed whether the Second Amendment guarantees a right to bear a sawed-off shotgun (Mr. Miller's specific situation) and not whether the Second Amendment guarantees the right to bear arms (the bigger issue of gun ownership). According to them, the bigger issue of whether the Second Amendment protects an individual's right to carry a gun is still unresolved. And, as was the case in Miller, when the Supreme Court does not indicate whether its ruling is specific to the facts or more general in scope, lower courts often come up with different interpretations.

Tools of Constitutional Interpretation Used in United States v. Emerson

What process does a court use to interpret a document that was written over two hundred years ago? In Emerson, the Fifth Circuit Court of Appeals went through the following steps:

1. Overview of the Second Amendment

The Court outlined three different ways to interpret the Amendment. It then looked at decisions of other courts of appeal and scholarly papers to see how others had addressed the same issue.

2. Precedent Established by United States v. Miller

If a court of appeals is deciding a matter that has been addressed by the Supreme Court, then it must apply the relevant law of that case. That requirement is called, "following precedent" or "*stare decisis*" (a fancy Latin phrase that literally translates as "to stand by that which is decided"). In Emerson, the Fifth Circuit Court of Appeals was required to make sure that its decision was consistent with the precedent established by the Supreme Court's opinion in Miller.

3. What Does the Text Say?

Generally, if you want to understand what something means, you look at what it says. However, there are times when the text is vague (not clear in its meaning), ambiguous (subject to more than one meaning), or inconsistent (appears to mean one thing in one instance and something else in another instance). For example, the Emerson Court took three pages to analyze whether the use of the word "people" in the Constitution referred only to individuals.

4. History of the Amendment

The Court is always mindful of the history that surrounds any provision of the Constitution. In Emerson, the Court took over twenty full pages to review many aspects of the Amendment's history. Included in this analysis was what happened in numerous state conventions leading up to the signing of the Constitution; writings that appeared in various journals and newspapers at the time of the creation of the Constitution; statements of the men involved in creating the Constitution, such as James Madison (also referred to as the "Framer's intent"); political discussions that were documented in personal letters; and the work of scholars.

5. Other Methods–Structure, Fairness, Political Theory, and Social Policy

Although they were not specifically used in Emerson, courts will also look at various other factors. In certain cases, the structure of the Constitution will help to determine how to address an issue. For example, if a branch of the government has historically been granted a certain power, a court might favor that branch in a struggle between two branches. In other cases, achieving a fair result can be important, and we see examples of this when a court balances two competing interests that it recognizes as valuable. Since our country is based on the political system of democracy and the financial principle of capitalism, courts may base their decisions on these fundamental ideals. For example, it might favor supporting economic development over personal property rights. Finally, social policy can also play a role in a court's analysis, for example, protecting the interests of children.

Where We Stand Today

Is the Fifth Circuit right? In sixty-six years, the Supreme Court has never overruled them! Twelve circuit courts to one, and the debate over the Second Amendment rages on . . . or does it? From the perspective of the Supreme Court, the Second Amendment debate appears to be dead. Despite the lack of a ruling that specifically supports an individual's right to bear arms and the interpretation of twelve circuit courts, ownership of guns (at least of handguns) appears to be a settled question. Instead, the discussion about gun ownership happens in the political arena, where the debate is about what types of guns people should be allowed to carry rather than whether they are allowed at all.

Hold the press! Despite years of little movement on this issue, at the time of this writing the District of Columbia Court of Appeals ruled that the Second Amendment applies to the individual (and not the states) when it invalidated a D.C. gun ownership ban. And this one could easily be headed to the U.S. Supreme Court. Stay informed and go to whywellwin.com for more info.

Federalism, the Tenth Amendment, and the Brady Bill: One Final Note

Our Constitution recognizes two independent spheres of government: federal and state. The concept of this dual structure is expressed in the Tenth Amendment:

> "The powers not delegated to the United States by the Constitution, nor prohibited by it to the States, are reserved to the States respectively, or to the people."

In regular language that means the federal government is only given the powers specified in the Constitution (a government of limited or "enumerated" powers), and all other powers are left either to the states or to the people.

The purpose of this structure is to prevent each government from taking too much power. If you think this sounds familiar, kind of like separation of powers and checks and balances, give yourself a star! Federalism is another mechanism that is built into the structure of the Constitution in order to ensure an even balance of power . . . and here's how it relates to gun control.

In 1993, Congress enacted the Brady Act (Jim Brady was President Reagan's Press Secretary and was shot in the attempted assassination of President Reagan). One of the goals of the Brady Act was to implement a national system to check the background of individuals seeking to purchase guns. Since it was going to take some time to put this program together, the Act set up an interim system that required the participation of the highest-ranking police official in each area. These individuals, identified as CLEOs (Chief Legal Enforcement Officers), were required to perform background checks to determine whether an individual attempting to buy a gun met federal guidelines. (Under the Gun Control Act of 1968, numerous groups of people could not legally own a gun: minors under twenty-one, convicted felons, fugitives, individuals committed to mental institutions, people dishonorably discharged from the military, and illegal aliens). The CLEOs were supposed to report this information to the retailer making the sale.

Two CLEOs filed suit to avoid having to participate in the federal program (Printz v. United States, 1997). Their argument was that the U.S. Constitution does not grant the federal government the authority to control state employees. And because all CLEOs work for the cities, towns, municipalities–all branches of the state government–they cannot be required to perform background checks to see if prospective buyers are eligible to own a gun under *federal* guidelines. Why? One word: Federalism.

Federalism means that the federal government's power is limited to federal matters. While the federal government could create its own administrative department or use an existing federal department–like the FBI–it could not require *state employees* to do this work for them, even on a temporary basis. The court agreed with the two CLEOs that the Brady Act allowed the federal government to "commandeer" state government employees in violation of the principle of federalism. And this part of the law was struck down.

ESSAY

Wayne LaPierre

CEO and Executive Vice President, National Rifle Association

The Second Amendment guarantees: "A well regulated Militia, being necessary to the security of a free State, the right of the people to keep and bear Arms, shall not be infringed."

To the Founding Fathers a civilian population that is protected from the threat of disarmament contributes to "the security of a free state" in two principal ways: self-defense, and protection of the republic through a citizen militia.

An armed citizenry is much less dependent on the

government for protection from the hazards of everyday life, both in a world (like that of the eighteenth century) where organized police forces did not exist, and in a world (like ours) in which the police can almost never put a stop to crimes in progress. The government is not constitutionally obligated to prevent crime. One federal court reminded that "there is no constitutional right to be protected by the state against being murdered by criminals or madmen."[1] As the Founding Fathers were well aware, the right of civilians to arm themselves enables citizens to exercise their fundamental, natural right to self-defense when they are threatened with criminal attack.

The most reliable studies indicate that armed civilians defend themselves against criminal violence over two million times each year.[2] Simply displaying a weapon is almost always sufficient to stop an attack, though armed civilians (who far outnumber the police) also shoot many more criminals than the police do.[3] In addition, the widespread civilian ownership of firearms in the United States creates powerful deterrent effects on criminal activity. Burglaries of occupied dwellings, for example, are rare in the United States compared with Great Britain.[4] The recent wave of liberalized concealed-carry laws has produced dramatic declines in violent crime in Texas and the other states that have adopted this policy.[5] Among the greatest beneficiaries of this policy have been women (who are more physically vulnerable than men) and minorities (who tend to live in areas where violent crime rates are higher).[6]

Secondly, the Founding Fathers trusted an armed citizenry as the best safeguard against the possibility of a tyrannical government. The very existence of an armed citizenry and its ability to form a citizen militia will tend to discourage would-be tyrants from attempting to "pacify" the population. This is not and could not be a guarantee against tyranny, but it surely raises the risks and costs of a tyrannous pacification, and thereby reduces the probability of its being attempted.[7]

James Madison, author of the Second Amendment, wrote that Americans had "the advantage of being armed" that was lacking in other nations, where "the governments are afraid to trust the people with arms." Patrick Henry proclaimed the "great object is that every man be armed . . . Everyone who is able may have a gun." The Second Amendment was then, as it is today, about freedom and the means to protect it.

In United States v. Miller, 307 U.S. 174 (1939), the Supreme Court refused to take judicial notice that a short-barreled shotgun was useful for militia purposes. Nowhere did the court hold that an individual does not have a right to keep and bear arms. In United States v. Gomez[8], Judge Kozinski opined that "the Second Amendment embodies the right to defend oneself and one's home against physical attack." In United States v. Hutzell[9], the court held that ". . . an individual's right to bear arms is constitutionally protected, see United States v. Miller." Emerson,[10] the court examined United States v. Miller and held: "We reject the collective rights and sophisticated collective rights models for interpreting the Second Amendment. We hold, consistent with *Miller*, that it protects the right of individuals . . . to privately possess and bear their own firearms."

The U. S. Supreme Court has recently recognized the Second Amendment as an important individual right.[11]

On December 17, 2004, the U.S. Department of Justice published an exhaustive Second Amendment memorandum. It concludes without reservation that "the Second Amendment secures a personal right of individuals, not a collective right that may only be invoked by a State or a quasi-collective right restricted to those persons who serve in organized militia units."[12]

The Founding Fathers distrusted a government that

wouldn't trust its people. To fulfill the promise of the Declaration of Independence, the authors of the U.S. Constitution and its Bill of Rights made it clear that individual rights were paramount. The Bill of Rights, wrote Madison, was "calculated to secure the personal rights of the people."

Some claim that banning only certain firearms does not constitute an infringement of Second Amendment rights. That measured ploy is not new. George Mason exposed it at Virginia's constitutional convention in 1788: "[W]hen the resolution of enslaving America was formed in Great Britain, the British Parliament was advised by an artful man . . . to disarm the people; that it was the best and most effectual way to enslave them; but that they should not do it openly, but weaken them, and let them sink gradually."

Our founders risked their lives to create a free nation, and they guaranteed freedom as the birthright of American citizens through the Bill of Rights. The Second Amendment remains the first right among equals, because it is the one we turn to when all else fails.

[1] *Bowers v. DeVito*, 686 F.2d 616, 618 (7th Cir. 1982).

[2] Gary Kleck & Marc Gertz, *Armed Resistance to Crime: The Prevalence and Nature of Self Defense with a Gun*, 86 J. Crim. L. & Criminology 150, 164 (1995).

[3] Gary Kleck, *Targeting Guns: Firearms and their Control* 162, 163 (Aldine de Gruyter 1997).

[4] *Id.* at 183.

[5] John R. Lott, Jr., *More Guns, Less Crime: Understanding Crime and Gun Control Laws* (University of Chicago Press 1998).

[6] *Id.* at 60-70.

[7] *See, e.g.*, Sanford Levinson, *The Embarrassing Second Amendment*, 99 Yale L.J. 637, 657 & n.96 (1989).

[8] 81 F.3d 846, 850 n. 7 (9th Cir. 1996).

[9] 217 F.3d 966, 969 (8th Cir. 2000).

[10] 270 F.3d 203 (5th Cir. 2001).

[11] *Planned Parenthood v. Casey*, 505 U.S. 833 (1992); *United States v. Verdugo-Urquidez*, 494 U.S. 259 (1991).

[12] http://www.usdoj.gov/olc/20040pinions.htm

AFFIRMATIVE ACTION

OUR SOCIAL HISTORY IS FULL OF EXAMPLES OF RACISM, sexism, ageism, and virtually every other type of "ism" one can imagine. One goal of our legal system is to prevent these injustices and the unequal treatment that goes with them . . . except, of course, for a few glaring exceptions like slavery and the failure to acknowledge women's rights for about 150 years. But the concept of equality in the Constitution–Equal Protection under the Fourteenth Amendment–does not mean that everyone is always treated the same. In fact, laws often treat people unequally. For example, laws that require men and not women to register for the military draft are clearly unequal. Drinking laws and driving laws treat minors and adults differently. Immigration and tax laws treat American citizens and legal aliens differently.

The key to understanding equal protection (EP) is recognizing *when* unequal treatment is legal and *why* it is allowed. But determining the "whens" and "whys" is not straightforward. Like many other areas of the law, equal protection requires the application of a test that has evolved through the years.

The EP test had a rather humble start. Its roots sprung up in what law school students are told is the most famous footnote in all of legal history: Footnote 4 of U.S. v. Carolene Products (1938). It was the first time the U.S. Supreme Court acknowledged that certain minority groups were not equally protected through the traditional political process. In almost a "gee, this might be a good idea" kind of way, the footnote suggested that laws affecting these groups–"discrete and insular minorities"–might require the application of a more rigorous standard. It was the Court's recognition that it could play a role in remedying this injustice.

Two Parts of Equal Protection

Before we look at how the Court responded to this moment of awareness, it is important to understand the injustice the Court was attempting to address. Most of the "isms," racism and sexism in particular, have one thing in common: They all discriminate based on a characteristic that people cannot change–usually skin color or gender. In legal speak these characteristics are called "immutable" or unchangeable. Generally, laws that treat people based on unchangeable qualities offend our sense of fairness. How can people receive equal protection if the law treats them differently based on characteristics that are fixed? Perhaps unequal treatment would be fine if it was based on qualities that people *could* change, like skills or education. But laws based on unchangeable qualities such as race are "offensive," "odious," "invidious," or just plain evil. That gives us our first concept.

Concept One: Laws Based on Unchangeable Qualities Are Evil

In evaluating EP laws, courts look at whether individuals are "similarly situated." Similarly situated means that people are in the same position relative to one another. For example, all professional golfers competing in a tournament are similarly situated. They all qualified for the tourney and are all equally positioned to win the prize money. And all people applying for a job may also be similarly situated. They are all new applicants and have an equal opportunity to compete for the position.

But twist things a little. Assume that two people are applying for a job, but one person is currently working for the company while the other is not. Assume that the company has a policy of giving preference to existing employees. Given the company's hiring policy, one person has a better chance of getting the job. Under these circumstances, the current employee and the outside person are not similarly situated in relation to the job. And that gives us our second piece of the EP equation.

Concept Two: Equality Applies Only to People That Are Similarly Situated

Combine these two components and . . .

Equal protection is violated when a law treats similarly situated individuals differently and this difference in treatment is based on an unchangeable characteristic.

Recognize what is *not* in this definition. Discrimination can still be okay if *either* two people are not similarly situated *or* the discrimination is based on a quality that is changeable–such as economic status or intelligence.

When and Why Is Discrimination Legal?

So when is discrimination legal? From the cases that followed Carolene Products, the Court ultimately developed three separate tests to evaluate whether a law meets the constitutional standard for equal protection–Strict Scrutiny, Intermediate Scrutiny, and Rational Basis Review. With different standards to choose from, the obvious question is which test gets applied in what cases? Since the goal is to protect specific groups of people, the test that courts apply depends upon the group being discriminated against. As a result, laws that raise an equal protection issue can be mapped out as follows:

- Race (Ethnic Origin or Nationality)–Strict Scrutiny: The most difficult test, and laws only pass this standard in special circumstances.
- Gender–Intermediate Scrutiny: Not as tough as Strict Scrutiny, but still very difficult for the law to pass this requirement.
- Any other group–Rational Basis review: A relatively low standard in which any "rational" reason is sufficient.

With that basic description, we can turn to the specific issue of Affirmative Action (AA). AA can take many forms, because an AA program can be designed to help ethnic minorities, women, people with physical handicaps, or virtually any other group. We'll look at a race-based program, because this issue gets significant national media attention.

In Plessy v. Ferguson (1892), Homer Plessy violated a Louisiana law that required separate rail cars for blacks and whites. In 1896, the U.S. Supreme Court held that separate facilities based on race were allowable under the equal protection clause of the Constitution as long as each group had similar quality facilities. The concept of "separate but equal" officially became the law of the land . . . that is, until the infamous case of Brown v. Board of Education (1954).

In Brown, black children were denied admission to a public school that was attended by white children. Although the facilities, teachers, and curricula were apparently the same at both the white and black schools, it was shown that black children saw a separate school as a stigma or sign of inferiority. Based upon this evidence, the Court acknowledged that "separate but equal" was, in fact, not equal. Convinced that separation was actually contributing to a feeling of inequality–because allowing it in schools gave the appearance of "institutional endorsement"–the Court reversed its position. Brown marked the end of legalized racial separation (although, in practice, it continued for many years).

Equal Protection in Schools–The "Plus Factor" System

The University of Michigan Law School is one of the nation's elite law schools. It currently ranks in the top ten in all major polls. In 1996, Ms. Barbara Grutter, a white applicant, applied for admission. After initially being placed on a wait list, she was rejected. She sued the School for discrimination, arguing that the School's admissions policy was racially biased. Specifically, she claimed that the Constitution requires equal treatment for all applicants (because they are similarly situated), and the School's admissions policy treated her, as a white applicant (an unchangeable characteristic), differently than minority applicants. In Grutter v. Bollinger (2003), the Supreme Court considered the admissions policy of the University of Michigan Law School (Bollinger was the President of the University of Michigan).

The Law School receives many more applicants than it has spots available–about 3500 applications for 350 spots, according to the Court. Like most law schools, the School's primary consideration is GPA (grade point average) and LSAT (law school admissions test) scores. In addition to these numbers, the School considers the applicant's undergraduate school, an optional personal statement, work experience, life experience, the potential for the applicant to contribute to the educational environment, and other criteria. Grutter argued that based on a comparison of her scores to others who were admitted, she also should have been admitted.

The School will consider a student's overall application, but all students must meet the School's minimum academic requirements to be offered a place. Although the School wants students who ultimately will do well in school and in their law practice, one of the stated goals of the admissions program is to create a "diverse" academic environment. Although not explicitly defined, diversity probably includes varied economic backgrounds, unique personal experiences, students from around the country and foreign students, a range of ages, and other factors. One type of diversity the School certainly focuses on is racial diversity.

In creating a diverse student body, the School considers identification with a minority racial group a "plus factor" in a student's application (more on the details of the "plus factor" system in a minute). According to the School, the "plus factor" system contributes to diversity by enrolling a "critical mass of minority students" that have historically been discriminated against. For purposes of admission, that specifically includes African-Americans, Hispanics, and

Native Americans. So, what is a "critical mass?" That's a good question, and one that never really gets answered. The School states that critical mass is "meaningful numbers" or "meaningful representation" of minority students. Again, that's not much help. One could reasonably guess that one to two students out of a class of one hundred are probably not meaningful, whereas twelve to fifteen might be. But either way, diversity is one of the School's goals, and it is achieved by specifically considering race as a factor.

Any public university is an arm of the State, and any policy of the Law School is considered an action of the State of Michigan. When that policy employs a racial classification, it raises immediate concerns because it is presumed to violate equal protection. So, what is required for a state law that clearly demonstrates a racial preference to meet with the Court's approval? Two words: Strict Scrutiny. In constitutional terms, Strict Scrutiny is really the test of all tests. It is applied in cases that touch on equal protection and, as mentioned in the Fundamental Rights Primer, when a law infringes upon a fundamental right.

The High Hurdle of Strict Scrutiny

Strict Scrutiny requires a two-part test:
Part 1. The law must be "necessary" to achieve a "compelling interest."
Part 2. The law must be "narrowly tailored," meaning that it must be crafted in a way that has as little negative impact as possible (in this case, minimizing the adverse effect on other applicants).

Just so you get the complete picture, here's what Intermediate Scrutiny and Rational Basis mean.

Intermediate Scrutiny requires a test that is very similar:
Part 1. The law must be "substantially related" to an "important interest."
Part 2. The law must be "narrowly tailored."

Rational Basis requires only a minimal test:
Part 1. The law must be "rationally related" to a "legitimate" government interest.
Part 2. The law must be "rational."

Strict Scrutiny, Intermediate Scrutiny, and Rational Basis, Part 1–The Interest

In each test, Part 1 actually has two components, both of which go from hard to easy to meet. The significance or importance of the interest goes from "compelling" to "important" to merely "legitimate." How closely the law is tied to that interest goes from "necessary" to "substantially related" to simply "rationally related." When you put these two parts together, you see that fewer laws will meet the requirement of "necessary to achieve a compelling interest" compared to those that need only be "rationally related to a legitimate interest." Generally, national security and protecting your constitutional rights are the only types of "compelling" interests that meet this part of the test.

Strict Scrutiny, Intermediate Scrutiny, and Rational Basis, Part 2–Narrow Tailoring: The Connection Between the Law and the Behavior

Tailoring looks at how closely the law addresses the behavior it is attempting to restrict. Both Strict and Intermediate Scrutiny require that the law is "narrowly tailored," whereas the Rational Basis standard simply requires that it is "rational." One way in which a court evaluates tailoring is by looking at whether the law is "over-inclusive" (impacts more people than is necessary) or "under-inclusive" (impacts fewer people than necessary).

Here's an example of narrow tailoring: take a law that attempts to minimize drug-related car crashes by requiring all teenagers to take a drug test in order to get a driver's license. This law is under-inclusive (includes fewer people than it should) because it doesn't test other drivers that may take drugs, namely, adults. It is also over-inclusive (includes more people than it should) because not all teenagers take drugs, and the law should be more narrowly focused on teenagers with prior drug-related arrests. Because the law is both under and over-inclusive, a court would likely find that this law is not narrowly tailored.

Back to Affirmative Action. How does AA fare against Strict Scrutiny's two-part test?

Part 1–Is "Diversity" a Compelling Interest?

The School claims that diversity, bringing together people with different experiences, backgrounds and points of view, supports the School's educational mission. The School also believes that it would not be able to achieve diversity without considering a wide variety of factors. And race is one of those factors.

PLEASANTVILLE
ELEMENTARY CELEBRATES
"DIVERSITY WEEK"
DIVERSITY GIVES US A CHANCE TO CELEBRATE EACH OTHERS' DIFFRENCES. WHAT MAKES US SPECIAL AND UNIQUE.
SO WHOSE FAMILY IS FROM ANOTHER COUNTRY?
HOW ABOUT ANOTHER STATE?
TOWN?
WELL THIS IS GUNNA BE A SHORT WEEK.

In Grutter, the Court does not challenge the School's claim that diversity, racial or otherwise, is something that should be pursued. As a result, the Court does not compare diversity to other possible purposes. Instead, the Court accepts the School's judgment. The Court plainly states, "The Law School's educational judgment that such diversity is essential to its educational mission is one to which we defer."

Did the Court punt? Did they avoid the tough question by not comparing diversity to other purposes? If you think so then consider the challenge in making that comparison. How would one measure the goal of diversity to the goal of admitting the best student? Or creating the most talented lawyers? Or creating the fairest admissions process? The School would likely answer that diversity contributes to all three goals. Without diversity, you won't have the best students, the most talented lawyers or the fairest system. You can see that comparing goals is tough, maybe even impossible, which might explain why the Court simply agreed. Bottom line–the Constitution recognizes that diversity is a valid goal in an educational setting.

Part 2–Is the "Plus System" Narrowly Tailored?

The School claims that the plus system is a narrowly

tailored way for the School to achieve student diversity. Neither the Court nor the School explains exactly how the plus system works, but the Court's opinion does a good job of explaining what this system is *not.* For example, we know it's not a quota system. The Court cites Regents of the University of California v. Bakke (1978), where the University of California at Davis Medical School set aside eight places out of fifty for minority applicants. The Bakke Court ruled that this program violated equal protection because it did not allow all students to compete for all open spots.

Additionally, we know that a school cannot have a preset point "bonus" for racial minority applicants. The Court cites Gratz v. Bollinger (decided the same day as Grutter v. Bollinger and, coincidentally, also brought against the University of Michigan). In Gratz, the Court evaluated the University's undergraduate admissions policy. The University automatically awarded minority applicants with twenty miscellaneous points out of a total one hundred possible points. The Court held that automatically awarding a significant percentage of the total points based on any one factor (in this case, race), made race a "decisive factor" in the admissions process and thus unacceptable.

The take-away from Bakke and Gratz is that equal protection requires that each applicant receive an individual evaluation. Whether that actually happens is determined by looking at the way a school weights its admissions factors. The program is legitimate if no factor is given too much weight. For example, a quota system fails because it makes race the only factor for a certain number of spots. And a "twenty out of one hundred" point system fails because, although not as lopsided as a quota, it still gives too much weight to one factor. The University of Michigan Law School's "plus system" is narrowly tailored because it is neither a quota nor does it weight race too heavily.

If you think the line's a little fuzzy, well, it is. We know that twenty points out of one hundred fails. How about ten points out of one hundred? Five points? Nobody knows. Despite its best intentions, the law, like life, can be fuzzy. But hopefully you recognize the Court's attempt to justify what it believes is a valid, constitutionally protected concept (whether you agree with the concept or the reasoning behind it is an entirely different question).

Think of it this way . . .

Think of the School's decision-making process in the same way as your personal decision-making process in selecting a life mate. Like the School, you weight factors: intelligence, attractiveness, family history, kissing ability, and, of course, personal issues. Imagine the Court is saying that you can give attractiveness more weight, but you can't base your decision on that one factor alone. Family history and personal issues must be considered as well. In the case of the School, race can be influential in the decision but not so much that it becomes the deciding factor.

The Dissent

There were several strong dissenting opinions in this decision, each criticizing aspects of the School's evaluation process. Here are three of their arguments:

1. "Critical mass" is a sham because it is not being applied evenly under any rationale (for example, in proportion to society or evenly among races). There are twice as many African American as Hispanic students in the School, which implies that critical mass is different for each group. Since there is no offered

justification for critical mass being applied differently to African American and Hispanic students, critical mass is simply a useless label.

2. Critical mass violates the Constitution because critical mass hides the true goal of the admissions program: the School has a target percentage of minority students it is trying to enroll (like a quota). Statistical evidence suggests that the target was between 12 and 14 percent during 1987–1990 and again during 1995–1998, with an increase to 19 to 20 percent from 1991–1994. The consistency of these numbers over several periods seems more than just coincidental. In fact, it is reasonable to conclude that the School was setting, and then adjusting, a target for minority students.

3. At the end of the admissions process, the School is potentially using race as a primary factor. The School uses daily reports to track students who have accepted the School's offer to attend. At the end of the acceptance process, when only a few spots are still open, the School may be choosing based almost entirely on race in order to achieve critical mass. If race is either the primary factor or possibly the only factor at this stage, then this process violates the need for individual consideration of each applicant.

In each of these arguments the dissent focuses on

the actual admissions process the School employs to achieve its goal. By taking this approach, the dissent does not address the more basic issue of whether Affirmative Action is ever justified. It simply makes the point that the particular approach used by the School does not pass equal protection.

Where Does This Leave Us?

The Court has ruled that racial diversity is a valid goal that schools can pursue in their admissions policies. Specifically, race can be a factor or "plus factor," as long as every candidate is individually considered. The Law School's "plus factor" system means that race gets an emphasis but not enough to make it the decisive factor. Most critically, the system still assures that each applicant gets the individual review that is required under equal protection. As a result, an Affirmative Action program that uses a "plus system" is constitutional under the Equal Protection Clause of the Fourteenth Amendment.

Affirmative Action in Government Contracts

In 1980, the Court was asked to decide the constitutionality of a Federal Public Works program that gave out $4 billion in grants to state and local governments for public works (construction) projects (Fullilove v. Klutznick). The law had an MBE (minority business enterprise) provision that required that 10 percent of each grant be spent with a minority business. An MBE was defined as a business that was at least 50 percent owned by minority group members or, if the company was public, minorities owned 51 percent of its stock. Minority group members were "citizens of the United States who are Negroes, Spanish-speaking, Orientals, Indians, Eskimos, and Aleuts."

The Court determined that the law was constitutional, and it cited several reasons: (1) Congress has the power to give money based on the recipient meeting certain conditions (for example, giving money to states for federal highways on the condition that they comply with driving regulations). (2) Congress found that there was a history of racial discrimination in contracts awarded to minority businesses (with

> no apparent shortage of qualified MBEs). (3) The program was short-term and the 10 percent was a "remedial" measure (meaning that the 10 percent set-aside was an attempt to remedy the past discrimination). (4) There was an "administrative waiver" in specific instances where it was not possible to meet the 10 percent requirement.

An Interesting Twist

Another area where affirmative action plays a critical role is in the U.S. Military. When the Supreme Court hears cases, various groups submit "friends of the court" briefs known as "amicus" briefs. In Grutter, one brief was from "former high-ranking officers and civilian leaders of the Army, Navy, Air Force, and Marine Corps." Of these twenty-nine men, fourteen had received Four Stars, three others were U.S. Senators, and two others served as Secretary of Defense, while the remainder had equally distinguished military careers. Their brief argues that limited race-conscious policies are necessary in order to build an effective military force. It explains how each branch of the armed forces uses race-based recruiting to achieve their specific affirmative action goals. Here are some direct excerpts from their brief:

"In Vietnam, racial tensions reached a point where there was an inability to fight . . . African-American troops, who rarely saw members of their own race in command positions, lost confidence in the military as an institution . . . Ultimately, the military of the 1970s recognized that its race problem was so critical that it was on the verge of self-destruction . . . There is presently no workable alternative to limited, race-conscious programs to increase the pool of qualified minority officer candidates and establish diverse educational settings for officer candidates . . . In the interest of national security, the military must be selective in admissions for training and education for the officer corps, and it must train and educate a highly qualified, racially diverse officer corps in a racially diverse educational setting . . . Today, there is no race-neutral alternative that will fulfill the military's and the nation's compelling need for a diverse officer corps of the highest quality to serve the country." (Notice how the interest is "compelling," and there is no "race-neutral alternative"–it's narrowly tailored).

" . . . Minorities are consistently offered admission to West Point at higher rates than whites despite lower academic predictor scores and lower academic, physical education, and military grades . . . Like West

Point, the U.S. Naval Academy . . . employs a limited race-conscious admissions policy . . . (and the) Naval Academy GAO Report further found that a higher percentage of minorities who did qualify were admitted to the Academy than their white counterparts . . . the Air Force will develop affirmative action programs which represent minorities, women, and persons with disabilities at all grade levels . . . the ROTC employs an aggressive race-conscious admissions program . . . the ROTC's recruiting programs and strategies are overtly race conscious."

Conclusion

In Grutter, one Justice points out that if a state can make race a factor in a publicly funded educational institution, then by the same logic it should also make those same distinctions with its state employees (because they are both state agencies). That is probably not likely to happen. In fact, the Court has not indicated that the goal of diversity or the use of race as a plus factor could be applied to other publicly funded organizations. Most likely, Affirmative Action will be limited to the area of education. However, this chapter should raise some interesting questions about how affirmative action applies in other areas.

Footnote

There are currently two cases in front of the Supreme Court regarding the use of race as a basis for admission to public elementary and high schools (Meredith v. Jefferson County Board of Education and Parents Involved in Community Schools v. Seattle School District). These school districts use race as the sole factor in admitting children in order to achieve racially balanced student bodies. This policy is being evaluated in light of the standard established in Grutter and the other Affirmative Action cases. Check the website at whywellwin.com and stay tuned for those developments.

ESSAY

Ward Connerly

Former U. of California Regent

"Affirmative action" is one of the most amorphous terms in American public policy. Yet for decades, this policy, practice, concept–whatever one wants to call it–was accepted almost without challenge. Not because all Americans embrace it, but because of the presumption that it was a beneficial effort to advance the movement of women and "minorities," especially black people, into the mainstream of American life.

On July 20, 1995, the Board of Regents of the University of California became the first public agency in the nation to prohibit race-based "affirmative action"–the application of different standards–in admissions, employment, and contracting.

On November 6, 1996, the voters of California applied this prohibition against race-based preferential treatment to all government agencies in California when they approved Proposition 209 by a margin of 55 to 45 percent. This initiative was a mirror image of the 1964 Civil Rights Act, because of its command that all citizens be treated equally "without regard to" race and skin color instead of treated differently because of those factors.

As the author of the resolutions (SP-1 and SP-2) adopted by the Regents, and the chairman of the Proposition 209 campaign, there were several factors guiding the actions that I provoked, which were ultimately approved by my colleagues and the people of California.

No one can deny that "black" people have endured considerable mistreatment throughout their history in America–enslavement, denial of the right to vote, segregated from the rest of society, forced to perform the most menial of jobs, denied access to public education, denied the right to use public accommodations–such as lunch counters and restrooms–and discriminated against in the housing market.

In its original form, the purpose of "affirmative action" was to ensure that black people would have access to American public life "without regard to race, color, or creed." Few individuals of goodwill quarrel with this objective. When President John F. Kennedy mentioned "affirmative action" in his 1961 executive order, he did so with the clear intent of expanding "civil rights" to include black Americans, not to limit the civil rights of other Americans. Over the years, however, a "tool" that has its origins in eradicating discrimination and providing access to black people has become a method of granting preferential treatment to "women and minorities" on the oft-spoken premise that America is controlled by white males and, thus, what would otherwise be considered discriminatory conduct is permissible in the interest of achieving "diversity."

We often forget that at the core of the American way of life is a profound sense of decency. As Americans, we are fundamentally decent people who want to do the right thing whenever we are confronted with a choice between right and wrong. Sometimes, we make mistakes with regard to how our government deals with its citizens. Nonetheless, we constantly move forward toward that "more perfect union."

It was in recognition of this sense of national decency that Dr. Martin Luther King, Jr., urged the American people to "live out the true meaning of your creed," as he led the effort to purge our nation of the oppressive conditions that confronted black people prior to and during that tumultuous period known as the "civil rights movement."

In 1963, shortly before his assassination, President John F. Kennedy said, "Race has no place in American life or law." The response of the nation to the vision of its fallen president, and to Dr. King and his eloquent vision of a nation where the color of a person's skin would not be a determining factor in that person's pursuit of happiness was clear and resounding: passage of the 1964 Civil Rights Act. This Act guaranteed that every American citizen would be treated "equally" in the public arena "without regard" to his or her race, skin color, or national ancestry.

The events beginning with Kennedy's executive order and culminating in passage of the Civil Rights Act firmly established the "colorblind" ethic as a basic

American civic value. We commemorate this value each year as we acknowledge the birthday of Martin Luther King, Jr. On this day, the memorable quote in which Dr. King yearns for an American future where his four little children will be judged by the "content of their character" instead of their skin color rings out across the land. Americans embrace this vision and equate it with "civil rights and the promise of America to every citizen. Treating citizens differently, in the guise of "affirmative action," soils that promise and makes "race" more–not less–of a factor in American life.

More than any other individuals, those harmed most by "affirmative action" are black people. They carry the stigma of being beneficiaries of preferential treatment because of the presumption of their "disadvantaged" status or their inability to compete; yet, to an ever-growing extent, black people benefit the least from such policies. Certainly, those who most require special consideration, low income, poorly educated blacks, do not benefit from affirmative action. Thus, we find the paradox of a program being created to ensure nondiscriminatory treatment of black people now benefiting black people minimally but discriminating against a host of others to advance recent immigrants (some illegal) and women.

"Affirmative action" has survived long past its life expectancy only because it has developed a cadre of individuals and organizations who are so heavily invested in its immortality that, like the die-hard segregationists, they simply refuse to let it go without a bitter fight. The fact that it represents a betrayal of one of our nation's basic civic values, namely that all of its citizens are of equal value in the eyes of the government; the fact that it is producing radically diminishing returns on the investment that is made into it; the fact that a growing list of individuals perceive themselves to be victims ("reverse discrimination") of this perverse system–none of this matters to its protectors.

These are the circumstances that have propelled the movement to end what began as a noble endeavor but which has tragically gone very wrong.

GAY MARRIAGE

LIKE SEVERAL ISSUES IN THIS BOOK, THE LEGAL DEBATE concerning gay marriage is about whether the Constitution recognizes a fundamental right that the state cannot deny. In this case, does the Constitution protect the right of two same-sex adults to marry?

What's at stake in this issue is more than just societal recognition that gay marriage is equivalent to "traditional" marriage. Equality is a precious social value, and it may be the most important motive for gay marriage advocates. But the legal outcome–whether federal and state governments would be required to provide the same rights and privileges as those accorded individuals in traditional marriages–also has very significant consequences.

What's at Stake?

The Vermont Supreme Court (Baker v. State of Vermont, 1999) summed up what's at stake for individuals who are denied the right to have a legal spouse. Here's what they said (paraphrased with conversational English in place of legal jargon):

"While the laws relating to marriage have undergone many changes during the last century, largely toward the goal of equalizing the status of husbands and wives, the benefits of marriage have not diminished in value. On the contrary, the benefits and protections incident to a marriage license under Vermont law have never been greater. They include, for example, the right to receive a portion of the estate of a spouse who dies without a will and protection against disinheritance through elective share provisions when your cheating, rich husband leaves you out of the will; preference in being appointed as the personal representative of a spouse who dies without a will; the right to bring a lawsuit for the wrongful death of a spouse; the right to bring an action for loss of consortium (a fancy word for the ability to have

> sex); the right to workers' compensation survivor benefits; the right to spousal benefits the State has guaranteed to public employees, including health, life, disability, and accident insurance; the opportunity to be covered as a spouse under group life insurance policies issued to an employee; the opportunity to be covered as the insured's spouse under an individual health insurance policy; the right not to testify against one's spouse; homestead rights and protections; the presumption of joint ownership of property and the right that it will pass to one's spouse upon death of the other; hospital visitation and other rights incident to the medical treatment of a family member; and the right to receive, and the obligation to provide, spousal support, maintenance, and property division in the event of separation or divorce."

Supporters of gay marriage argue that marriage should be defined broadly to include any relationship and not just that between a man and a woman. Opponents of gay marriage appear to fall into two camps: one camp believes that marriage should be traditionally defined and restricted to matrimony between a man and a woman. A second camp shares the traditional view of marriage but also accepts the idea of gay couples participating in legally recognized "civil unions."

The U.S. Supreme Court has never directly addressed the issue of whether the Constitution protects the right to same-sex marriage. Assuming that one day it elects to do so, there are several issues that might be examined. One is whether the right to marry someone of the same sex is a fundamental right. And if so, should gay marriage be treated like "traditional" marriage (which I will refer to from here forward as simply "marriage")? Another is whether gays are a protected minority and cannot be discriminated against because under the concept of equal protection the Constitution forbids discrimination against a protected class.

This chapter addresses the two issues relating to gay marriage and civil unions. First, we'll examine the question of whether marriage is a fundamental right and consider a case that will likely play a key role in determining how gay marriage fits within the U.S. Constitution. Second, we'll examine the concept of equal protection and how it's applied to laws about civil unions. This includes a discussion of how gay marriage played out in the State of Massachusetts, where a proposed law creating "civil unions" made its way through the State legislature and State Supreme Court.

Issue 1: Is Marriage a Fundamental Right?

If you had lived in Virginia in the 1960s, you might have been tuning in, turning on, and dropping out (to paraphrase Timothy Leary). But if you were a white man, you certainly were not marrying a black woman . . . at least not legally. Why? Because according to Virginia State law, it was a crime for "any white person in this State to marry any (except) a white person . . . 'white person' shall apply only to such person as has no trace whatever of any blood other than Caucasian." Virginia was one of sixteen states that prohibited interracial marriages. All these marriages were automatically void, and the punishment for this felony was a prison sentence of one to five years.

Loving v. Virginia (1967) featured an interracial couple, a black woman and a white man, against the State of Virginia. The Lovings were married in Washington D.C., and after moving back to Virginia, they were indicted for violating Virginia law. They pleaded guilty and were sentenced to one year in jail. At sentencing, the judge offered the couple with an alternative to jail time: He would suspend their sentence provided they left the state and did not return for twenty-five years. In other words, go to jail or leave the state. In explaining his sentence, the Judge stated, "Almighty God created the races, white, black, yellow, malay and red, and he placed them on separate continents. And but for the interference with his arrangement there would be no cause for such marriages. The fact that he separated the races shows that he did not intend for the races to mix." The State of Virginia's highest court–the Supreme Court of Appeals of Virginia–upheld their conviction.

On appeal, the U.S. Supreme Court reversed the Virginia Court's decision. The U.S. Supreme Court based its verdict primarily on the fact that the Constitution guarantees equal protection and forbids racial discrimination. Because the Virginia law treated people of different races differently, it did not even pass the lowest constitutional standard of Rational Basis–meaning that the State didn't even have a "rational" or "legitimate" reason for the law. Without a valid reason for the law, the Court had no need to fully examine the underlying issue of whether marriage was a fundamental right. Despite this, there are a few paragraphs that mention marriage, and some of these statements could provide insights into how the Court might one day interpret a case on gay marriage.

Position 1: The Loving Decision Supports the Argument for Gay Marriage

Specifically, the Court stated: "The freedom to marry has long been recognized as one of the vital personal rights *essential to the orderly pursuit of happiness* by free men . . . Marriage is one of the *basic civil rights of man, fundamental to our very existence* and survival."

When the Court describes a right in broadly sweeping terms such as a "basic civil right of man," it implies that it recognizes that right as fundamental (and, as mentioned, the Court has recognized marriage as a fundamental right). If the Court interpreted this language to apply to *any* type of marriage, including gay marriage, a government would have a difficult time justifying the restriction of gay marriage (since a fundamental right can only be denied when the law infringing upon that right passes Strict Scrutiny).

Position 2: Loving Does NOT Support the Argument for Gay Marriage

In the Loving decision, the Court also made statements that could be interpreted as not applying to gay marriage. It stated, "To deny this fundamental freedom on so unsupportable a basis as the *racial* classifications . . . The Fourteenth Amendment requires that the freedom of choice to marry not be restricted by invidious *racial* discriminations . . . the freedom to marry, or not to marry, a person of another *race* resides with the individual and cannot be infringed by the State."

Here, the Court is focusing on *race* discrimination. Because marriage is restricted in other ways–for example, laws prohibiting marrying a close relative–there is no reason why gay marriage couldn't simply be another legitimate restriction. And unless homosexuals are deemed a protected class, they would not be afforded any special protection (more on that under equal protection). Under this interpretation, Loving is about race and the case doesn't support the gay marriage argument.

As you can see, the question about how to interpret Loving, and whether it could be used to support gay marriage, is open to debate.

Issue 2: Equal Protection

Equal protection guarantees equal treatment under the law. As we saw in examining Affirmative Action, the only exception is when the class of people being discriminated against are "protected"–usually on the grounds of race or gender–and therefore entitled to additional safeguards. Based on how the Court has ruled in several other cases, it appears that the Court does not and likely would not consider homosexuals a protected class (if you want a refresher, see the chapter on affirmative action to understand how that determination is made).

The consequence of this is very significant. Laws that discriminate against *protected* groups must pass Strict Scrutiny. Under this rigorous standard, the state law must be "necessary in order to achieve a compelling purpose." In layman's terms, there must be a *very* good reason to justify the discrimination. As a result, such laws almost always fail. By comparison, laws that discriminate against *unprotected* groups only need to be "rational" to pass. Consequently, almost any non-discriminatory reason is sufficient to justify the law. That's why discrimination against *unprotected* groups is almost always allowed.

Quick Recap

First, is gay marriage a fundamental right like traditional marriage? If it is, then any law that impacts gay marriage must pass the Court's highest standard of

Strict Scrutiny, and that's not easy to do. If not, then it only needs to pass the lowest standard of Rational Basis, and most laws meet this requirement.

Second, are homosexuals a protected class under equal protection? If they are protected, then these laws must pass Strict Scrutiny ("necessary to achieve a compelling interest"). If not, then laws impacting them must only be "rational."

Despite the high level of respect that a court gives a state law when it applies the Rational Basis test, there are times when a court appears to add teeth to this otherwise easy to pass standard.

Romer v. Evans and Baker v. State of Vermont: Does Discrimination Against Homosexuals Meet the Minimal Requirements of the Rational Basis Test?

In 1996, the U.S. Supreme Court examined a Colorado Voter Amendment that altered the Colorado State Constitution (Romer v. Evans). The Amendment prevented any State agency, including the courts, from protecting against the discrimination of homosexuals. Specifically, the Amendment prevented State agencies from making rulings or decisions that protected "homosexual, lesbian, or bisexual orientation, conduct, practices, or relationships." The law did not apply to any other groups. In other words, the law singled out homosexuals and specified that they were not to be granted any special treatment.

The Romer Court found that the Amendment failed even the Rational Basis test because there was no legitimate reason for passing the law. In fact, the Court indicated that the law seemed to have been designed for the sole purpose of impacting the rights of one particular group. In explaining why the Amendment failed even the Court's least restrictive test, the Court remarked that under equal protection, "a bare desire to harm a politically unpopular group cannot constitute a legitimate governmental interest."

The dissent, however, viewed the issue differently. Under existing Colorado law, homosexuals are not a protected class. Accordingly, they are only entitled to the same protections as any other member of society. Just like laws that discriminate based on age, veteran status, and family status, discrimination against unprotected classes is allowable. In their view the Colorado law was not harmful; rather, it simply prevented State institutions from passing laws giving gays *preferential* treatment (for example, the law would have prevented a State university from extending fringe benefits to "life partners" unless this perk applied more generally to all roommates). According to the dissent, homosexuals could still make discrimination claims, but they simply could not base these claims on sexual orientation. In other words, the law only reinforced an existing State law.

Romer is a rare example where the Supreme Court made the standard of Rational Basis tougher to pass. This is the exception to the rule, since the Court can almost always find a "rational" reason for a legislature's decision to pass a law. However, if the Court were to take on a gay marriage case, then its treatment of Rational Basis would be critical to the outcome.

But surely marriage promotes family, creates offspring, and provides a host of other family-related benefits? Wouldn't any of these reasons be considered a rational reason that would enable a law to pass the Rational Basis standard?

Well, apparently not . . . at least not in Vermont. In 1999, several homosexual couples were denied marriage licenses and brought suit in a Vermont court (Baker v. State of Vermont). The State argued that gays could be denied a license because the State law had a valid purpose, including promoting "the link between procreation and marriage" and promoting "child rearing." The Vermont Supreme Court cited various reasons why these purposes did not even pass Rational Basis, including the fact that these reasons were in direct conflict with the State's policy of allowing gays to adopt children. The Court concluded that "none of the interests asserted by the State provides a *reasonable* basis for the exclusions of same-sex couples from the benefits [of marriage]." In other words, the existence of laws that apply to homosexuals–like permitting gay adoption–made it more difficult for the State to satisfy the Rational Basis standard and prohibit gay marriage.

With that background, we move on to what happened in Massachusetts.

Massachusetts: Marriage vs. Civil Unions

The State of Massachusetts has taken the issue of gay marriage through a lengthy judicial and legislative process. These events started with a case about whether same-sex marriage was legal under the Massachusetts State Constitution. The case was eventually appealed to the Massachusetts Supreme Court. Like the U.S. Supreme Court in the Loving decision, the Massachusetts Supreme Court focused its discussion on the fundamental right of marriage. And using language that was very similar, the Court concluded that denying marital rights to gay couples meant that homosexuals would be "excluded from the full range of human experience." The Court decided that the State constitution did not allow the State to prevent gay couples from getting married.

The legislature responded to the Court's decision by drafting a law that created two categories of marriage: "marriage" and "civil union." Under the proposed law, "marriage" was a label that applied to heterosexual couples that married, while "civil union" was the label given to homosexual couples that married. The law provided that "marriages" and "civil unions" carried all the same benefits, meaning that an individual in a gay civil union would be entitled to all the same health, tax, spousal, and other benefits and opportunities offered by the State that are available to an individual in a heterosexual marriage. Before the revised law was enacted, the legislature asked the Massachusetts Supreme Court to provide an "advisory opinion" about whether this new law was consistent with the State constitution. (The U.S. Constitution, unlike the Massachusetts Constitution, does not permit the U.S. Supreme Court to offer "advisory opinions" unless these opinions are tied directly to an actual case that is before the Court, and neither the U.S. Congress nor

President of the United States has the authority to ask the Supreme Court for advice.) The Massachusetts Supreme Court advised the State legislature that even the revised law failed to meet the requirements of equal protection under the State constitution.

Here are the pro and con arguments that appeared in their advisory opinion:

It's a BAD LAW: Two Labels Implies Unequal Protection

Equal protection requires equal treatment of similarly situated people. Although the law provides no difference in State benefits, the label of "civil union" creates a stigma. That stigma gives gay couples "second-class status." The "separate but equal" experiment was tried with school segregation . . . and, in case you forgot, it failed. You can have group classifications when they are based on *meaningful distinctions.* But, here, the State of Massachusetts even admits that its stated purpose of promoting procreation and child rearing do not justify creating two classes of married people, because the State already allows gay couples to adopt. So the proposed law fails to provide even a rational reason for its existence, and the discriminatory effect of the law violates equal protection.

It's a GOOD LAW: There Is a Genuine Basis for Distinction

We're not talking about separate but equal; we are talking about separate and unequal. There are several *meaningful differences* between gay and straight couples: First, gay couples will not have the same benefits as heterosexual couples. For example, federal tax credits will not apply to gay couples. Second, gay couples will not have their marriages recognized by other states. As a result, a gay couple cannot get divorced in another state, nor receive the same benefits that they would if they remained in Massachusetts. Third, Massachusetts will have to differentiate between homosexual and heterosexual couples for various administrative purposes. In short, there are very real and meaningful differences. And since this case does not present an argument that gay marriage is a fundamental right, the law does not need to meet the more demanding Strict Scrutiny test, and it only needs to pass Rational Basis. Because Rational Basis only requires "any rational reason," all the reasons offered by the legislature are more than sufficient to overcome this minimal standard.

Full Faith and Credit, DOMA, and the Same-Sex Marriage Amendment

Full Faith and Credit

Article IV of the U.S. Constitution requires that each state accept–give Full Faith and Credit to–the "public Acts, Records and judicial Proceedings of every other State." It's why you can sue your husband in California and collect on his New York bank account. In other words, it guarantees that with few exceptions each state will accept the decisions of sister states. In the area of marriage, it means that if you get legally married in Nevada, you can get legally divorced in Georgia two weeks later.

DOMA

The Defense of Marriage Act (DOMA) is a federal law that defines marriage as that between a man and a woman. It specifically allows any state to deny the marital rights that another state has granted to a homosexual couple. It contradicts the idea of Full Faith and Credit, which raises the issue of whether it violates the U.S. Constitution (a case that is making its way through the courts). As a result, a gay couple that gets "married" in Massachusetts can neither get divorced nor will their marriage be recognized in over two-thirds of the other states. A number of states have passed their own version of DOMA; here is Arkansas's:

"Marriage shall be only between a man and a woman. A marriage between persons of the same sex is void. All (legal out-of-state) marriages shall be valid in . . . this state. This section shall not apply to a marriage between persons of the same sex."

The Proposed Same-Sex Marriage Amendment to the United States Constitution

The Same-Sex Marriage Amendment says about the same thing as DOMA:

"Marriage in the United States shall consist only of the union of a man and a woman. Neither this [the U.S.] Constitution, nor the Constitution of any State, shall be construed to require that marriage or the legal incidents thereof be conferred upon any union other than the union of a man and a woman."

The important difference between the two is

this: DOMA only addresses the relationship between states, while the Marriage Amendment would alter the Constitution. If the Constitution was changed and marriage was defined as only between a man and a woman, then the issue would be settled. States could not even allow gay people to get married. They *might* be able to provide similar benefits under another name–such as civil unions–but not under the label of marriage.

Conclusion

So what does it all mean? It means that, for now, each state has the ability to decide whether to grant marital rights to gay couples. It also likely means that if a state allows gay marriage or civil unions, then a gay couple's marriage would not be recognized in another state (unless that state has also decided to recognize gay marriage). At present there does not seem to be enough momentum to pass an Amendment to the Constitution. It is also unclear whether the U.S. Supreme Court will enter this debate (although DOMA might bring about its participation). Arguably, the Supreme Court was not designed to resolve social issues, because those are better left to a democratic process that includes elected officials. On the other hand, this is a fundamental rights issue, and it's the Court's job to interpret the Constitution in an area of legal uncertainty. Stay tuned and head to whywellwin.com for updates.

ESSAY

Mitt Romney

Former Governor, Massachusetts

Same-sex marriage is a subject about which people have tender emotions, in part because it touches individual lives. It also has been misused by some as a means to promote intolerance and prejudice. This is a time when we must fight hate and bigotry, when we must root out prejudice, when we must learn to accept people who are different from one another. Like me, the great majority of Americans wish both to preserve the traditional definition of marriage and to oppose bias and intolerance directed towards gays and lesbians.

Given the decision of the Massachusetts Supreme Judicial Court, Congress and America now face important questions regarding the institution of marriage. Should we abandon marriage as we know it and as it was known by the framers of our Constitution?

Has America been wrong about marriage for two hundred plus years? Were generations that spanned thousands of years from all the civilizations of the world wrong about marriage? Are the philosophies and teachings of all the world's major religions simply wrong? Or is it more likely that four people among the seven that sat in a court in Massachusetts have erred? I believe that is the case.

And I believe their error was the product of seeing only a part, and not the entirety. They viewed marriage as an institution principally designed for adults. Adults are whom they saw in the courtroom. And so they thought of adult rights, equal rights for adults. If heterosexual adults can marry, then homosexual adults must also marry to have equal rights.

But marriage is not solely for adults. Marriage is also for children. In fact, marriage is principally for the nurturing and development of children. The children of America have the right to have a father and a mother.

Of course, even today, circumstances can take a parent from the home, but the child still has a mother and a father. If the parents are divorced, the child can visit each of them. If a mother or father is deceased, the child can learn about the qualities of the departed. His or her psychological development can still be influenced by the contrasting features of both genders. Are we ready to usher in a society indifferent about having fathers and mothers? Will our children be indifferent about having a mother and a father?

Marriage is about even more than children and adults. The family unit is the structural underpinning of all successful societies. And it is the single most powerful force that preserves society across generations, through centuries.

Scientific studies of children raised by same-sex couples are almost nonexistent. And the societal implications and effects on these children are not likely to be observed for at least a generation, probably several generations. Same-sex marriage doesn't hurt my marriage, or yours. But it may affect the development of children and thereby future society as a whole. Until we understand the implications for human development of a different definition of marriage, I believe we should preserve that which has endured over thousands of years.

Preserving the definition of marriage should not infringe on the right of individuals to live in the manner of their choosing. One person may choose to live as a single, even to have and raise her own child. Others may choose to live in same-sex partnerships or civil arrangements. There is an unshakeable majority of opinion in this country that we should cherish and protect individual rights with tolerance and understanding.

But there is a difference between individual rights and marriage. An individual has rights, but a man and a woman together have a marriage. We should not deconstruct marriage simply to make a statement about the rights of individual adults. Forcing marriage to mean all things will ultimately define marriage to mean nothing at all.

Some have asked why so much importance is attached to the word "marriage." It is because changing the definition of marriage to include same-sex unions will lead to further far-reaching changes that also would influence the development of our children. For example, school textbooks and classroom instruction may be required to assert absolute societal indifference between traditional marriage and same sex practice. It is inconceivable that promoting absolute indifference between heterosexual and homosexual unions would not significantly affect child development, family dynamics, and societal structures.

Among the structures that would be affected would be religious and certain charitable institutions. Those with scriptural or other immutable founding principles will be castigated. Ultimately, some may founder. We need more from these institutions, not less, and particularly so to support and strengthen those in greatest need. Society can ill afford further erosion of charitable and virtuous institutions.

This is not a mere political issue. It is more than a matter of adult rights. It is a societal issue. It encompasses the preservation of a structure that has formed the basis of all known successful civilizations. With a matter as vital to society as marriage, I am troubled when I see an intolerant few wrap the marriage debate with their bias and prejudice.

I am also troubled by those on the other side of the issue who equate respect for traditional marriage with intolerance. The majority of Americans believe marriage is between a man and a woman, but they are also firmly committed to respect, and even fight for civil rights, individual freedoms, and tolerance. Saying otherwise is wrong, demeaning, and offensive. As a society, we must be able to recognize the salutary effect, for children, of having a mother and a father while at the same time respecting the civil rights and equality of all citizens.

Excerpts of Testimony before the U.S. Senate Judiciary Committee

DEATH PENALTY

ALTHOUGH SOME BELIEVE THE DEATH PENALTY SHOULD be abolished altogether, courts have never come close to doing so. That's because the United States Constitution allows states to impose the death penalty . . . provided they do not violate the Eighth Amendment's ban on cruel and unusual punishment. Despite the clarity of the main issue, the Supreme Court has been very involved in attempting to define the details (how and when the death penalty may be applied). Based on these cases, states cannot put to death mentally retarded people, people who are insane, or children under eighteen years of age. States can impose the death penalty for certain types of murder, but cannot do so for robbery or rape.

As always, let's start with the text of the Constitution. The Eighth Amendment:

> "Excessive bail shall not be required, nor excessive fines imposed, nor cruel and unusual punishments inflicted."

If your first thought after reading this was, "Gee, that's kind of vague," then you are not alone. In this final chapter, it should be clear that much of the Constitution leaves a lot open to interpretation. The Supreme Court has interpreted the Eighth Amendment to apply to the legal *process* that each state goes through before putting someone to death. As a consequence, there are limits on which crimes qualify (as in, does the punishment fit the crime?), the role of the jury, and the appeals process. But the primary question raised by the phrase "nor cruel and unusual punishments inflicted" applies to the *methods* of execution that are prohibited.

What execution methods should be considered cruel and unusual? Since there is no clear-cut standard, courts have looked at whether particular punishments are "barbaric" or "inhumane." One way to evaluate whether a punishment is barbaric is to consider its goal.

Torturing someone to death, a form of punishment that clearly qualifies as barbaric, is considered cruel because its purpose is to cause pain during the process of killing. In contrast, killing someone by a method such as electrocution is not considered cruel because, although it may be painful, such pain is considered incidental to the goal of ending that person's life.

The Case of Willie Francis (Francis v. Resweber, 1947)

Willie Francis was convicted of murder in 1945 and sentenced to death by electrocution. Unfortunately for Mr. Francis, the wires to his chair had been improperly installed. As a result he was only severely shocked, and his electrocution failed. His attorney appealed the case to the U.S. Supreme Court, arguing that electrocuting someone twice was surely cruel and unusual punishment. Here is the Court's response:

"The fact that an unforeseeable accident prevented the prompt consummation of the sentence cannot, it seems to us, add an element of cruelty to a subsequent execution. There is *no purpose to inflict unnecessary pain* nor any unnecessary pain involved in the proposed execution.

> The situation of the unfortunate victim of this accident is just as though he had suffered the identical amount of mental anguish and physical pain in any other occurrence, such as, for example, a fire in the cell block. We cannot agree that the hardship imposed upon the petitioner rises to that level of hardship denounced as denial of due process because of cruelty."

Before we get too far into this topic, here's a little history for you to consider.

Why the Death Penalty Came About

The Virginia Colony has the distinction of administering the first execution in this country in 1608. At about the same time, the State of New York had a rather interesting list of death penalty crimes, including denial of the true God, sodomy, kidnapping, traitorous denial of the king's rights, conspiracy to invade other New York towns, and (my personal favorite) striking your mother or father.

Until the mid 1800s, executions were performed in public. In what sounds like the modern day equivalent of a rock concert, tens of thousands of people would watch hangings while local vendors sold alcohol and souvenirs. Fights would regularly break out and spectators would often tear down the gallows and ropes as mementos. Excited viewers would yell at the widows and heckle the family members of the condemned. In addition to hanging, states sometimes administered the death penalty by drawing and quartering (cutting the torso into four quadrants), disemboweling (taking out your bowels), and beheading. In an attempt to bring some civility to our newly established nation, the Framers created the Eighth Amendment to eliminate the inhumane and barbaric methods that states used to administer punishments.

Although the methods have been modified, the

practice of capital punishment has survived. In fact, because this practice has been used so consistently throughout our nation's history, the constitutionality of the death penalty was not even challenged for nearly two hundred years. But in the 1976 case of Gregg v. Georgia, the Court was asked to determine the status of the death penalty. Let's look at their decision.

Gregg v. Georgia: The Modern Day Interpretation

Troy Gregg was hitchhiking and was picked up by two men in a car. At a rest stop, Gregg brutally murdered both men, shooting one man in the eye and the other in the cheek and back of the head. Several days later, Gregg was apprehended while driving the car of one of the victims. He was tried and convicted of murder, and the jury recommended the death penalty. Gregg appealed his conviction, arguing that the death penalty violates the Eighth Amendment's ban on cruel and unusual punishment. He argued that society's view of the death penalty had evolved, and the notion of putting people to death was inconsistent with current moral values.

Gregg was not asking the Court to review a particular method of execution. He was asking the Court to decide whether a death sentence, as opposed to life in prison, was *ever* a legal punishment. The Court evaluated his argument based on two criteria.

Death Penalty Stats (2004)

- Total U.S. inmates in state and federal prisons–1,421,911
- U.S. prisoners under death sentence–3,314
- Total U.S. Executions–59
  - Racial Breakdown–36 White; 19 Black; 3 Hispanic; 1 Asian
- State with the most executions–Texas (23)
- Total worldwide executions (2005)–2,148
  1. China–1,770
  2. Iran–94
  3. Saudi Arabia–86
  4. United States–60
- Total prisoners executed 1976-2007–1079
- Death row prisoners released since 1973–124

Part 1: An Objective Measure

The Court attempted to objectively measure whether society's attitude towards the death penalty had changed. It did this by actually counting the number of states that had modified their death penalty position over a given period of time. A significant change in the position of a number of states would provide objective evidence of society's change in attitude.

Here's an example: Assume that twenty years ago the death penalty was legal and in use in forty states. Twenty years later the death penalty was still being used in only three states. This drastic change would indicate that society no longer believed that death should be a form of punishment. And if society no longer approved of this practice, then it could be banned under the Eighth Amendment.

However, as simple as this state counting approach appears, it introduces a major problem: the precise number of states and the time period required to establish this change is not clearly defined. For example, if ten states change their view within a three-year period, is this evidence of societal change? How about ten states over a seventy-year period?

In Gregg, thirty-five states over a four-year period passed legislation that supported using the death penalty. Those statistics were enough for the Court to determine that society still favored its use. By contrast, in Simmons, a case that applied the death penalty to juveniles under eighteen (the facts of the Simmons case are provided below), the Court relied upon radically different numbers. In Simmons, only four states over a fifteen-year period passed legislation outlawing the death penalty. Yet this change was enough to persuade a majority of the Court that society no longer supported putting people under eighteen years of age to death.

In the Simmons decision, several members of the Court expressed their dissatisfaction about the lack of a precise standard for determining whether society's views had changed. From their perspective, state counting without guidelines or some other clearly defined method was simply another way of justifying the implementation of one's personal view–and this is supposed to be an *objective* test. To illustrate their position, they pointed out the discrepancy between the numbers in Gregg and those in Simmons. Given this giant pitfall, they felt that the decision about which criminals should be subject to the death penalty was a choice best left to each individual state.

Part 2: A Subjective Gauge

The second part of the test that the Court uses to evaluate whether the death penalty meets the requirements of the Eighth Amendment is applying its own subjective judgment. Under this part of the test the Court determines whether a particular punishment is consistent with the underlying principles of our judicial system–our basic morality. The idea is not that each member of the Court applies his or her own personal judgment. Rather, they are supposed to evaluate whether society has evolved to the point where the Amendment applies independently of what states have done.

There are two primary purposes behind all forms of punishment in our judicial system that the Court must consider: deterrence and retribution.

Goal 1: Deterrence–discouraging people from committing crimes. The idea behind deterrence is straightforward: people will not participate in illegal activities if they are afraid of the consequences. In the case of the death penalty, people won't kill others if they know they might be put to death.

Goal 2: Retribution–society seeks revenge in order to prevent people from taking the law into their own hands.

Although these principles seem straightforward, applying them is not. The Court has virtually given up on using deterrence as a rationale to support the death penalty because numerous studies have failed to definitively conclude whether or not criminals are actually deterred. Deterrence probably works in some cases and not in others.

Dealing with retribution is not any easier. How is the Court supposed to evaluate whether applying the death penalty to eighteen-year-olds but not seventeen-year-olds satisfies society's desire for revenge? Aren't those decisions ultimately judgment calls–personal judgment calls?

In applying the subjective part of the test in its decisions, the Court has referred to social science studies, history, legal theories, and even treatment of these issues by foreign courts. It shouldn't be surprising that members of the Court who are troubled by the subjectivity of the state counting method are even less enthusiastic about this part of the test. Some of their frustration is fueled by what's at stake. If the Court finds that a particular form of punishment violates the Eighth Amendment (such as putting people under eighteen or mentally retarded people to death), then all states lose the right to apply that form of punishment.

In the case of Gregg, the number of states changing their position and the subjective judgment of the Justices meant that society still favored the death penalty. As one Justice said, "Whatever the arguments may be against capital punishment, both on moral grounds and in terms of accomplishing the purposes of punishment . . . the death penalty has been employed throughout our history, and, in a day when it is still widely accepted, it cannot be said to violate the constitutional concept of cruelty." Despite the ruling, the State of Georgia never put Mr. Gregg to death. Ironically, Gregg escaped from prison the night before his execution only to die in a bar fight later that same evening.

Quick Recap:
The death penalty has been around for a long time, and there appears to be a strong historical and legal foundation for its existence. However, the way the death penalty is applied is very much up for debate. The Court uses both an objective test and a subjective gauge as to whether a particular punishment meets with the Constitution's ban on cruel and unusual punishment. As a result, some groups of people and the perpetrators of certain types of crimes are ineligible for the death penalty.

An Experience with the Death Penalty System
–David Kaczynski

Up until 1995, my views on capital punishment were purely theoretical. I never imagined that one day I'd have a personal confrontation with the capital punishment system. But that fateful day came in September of 1995 when my wife Linda suggested that my estranged older brother Ted might be the notorious "Unabomber."

At first, I simply couldn't believe that Ted was capable of harming anyone. The Unabomber was responsible for a series of mail bombs that killed three people and injured numerous others over seventeen years. Although I believed that Ted was disturbed–he was eventually diagnosed with schizophrenia–I'd never seen any signs of violence in him. But as Linda and I pored over the Unabomber's published Manifesto, I began to confront the reality that my brother, Ted Kaczynski, might be the Unabomber.

We soon found ourselves facing a terrible dilemma where any choice we made could easily result in someone's death. If we did nothing, Ted might kill again. On the other hand, if we handed him over to the FBI, he could be executed. I asked myself what it would be like to go through life with my own brother's blood on my hands. All I wanted was to make a life-affirming choice, but the death penalty denied me that option.

Our decision to turn Ted in was based on the belief that we were morally obliged to do whatever we could to stop the violence. We held on to a desperate hope that Ted might be exonerated by the FBI's investigation; or, if not, that prosecutors might understand that Ted was a very sick human being, not an evil monster. But we were resolved to stop the violence no matter what. We could only hope that the justice system would behave in an equally principled way.

Over the next two years, I witnessed firsthand how the criminal justice system actually works. The U.S. Justice Department promised to protect our privacy. Instead we were swamped with media attention on the day of Ted's arrest and for months afterward, and personal information we shared in confidence with the FBI ended up in the *New York Times.* Prosecutors solemnly promised to make a "fair and impartial" evaluation of my brother's mental condition. Instead they found a notorious "hired gun" legal expert to provide psychiatric testimony in my brother's case.

I began to see the criminal justice system for what it is: an imperfect system run by fallible human beings. It is influenced by so many variables and so many subjective judgments that inconsistent results are practically guaranteed. Prosecutors pursue their own agendas heavily influenced by politics and bias. Police are reluctant to admit mistakes and, in some cases, are even corrupt. Forensic labs sometimes mishandle evidence and have been known to fudge results. The entire judicial system presumes a level playing field, but too often justice gets lost in the shuffle. As a result, we have a death penalty that disproportionately impacts the poor, the black, and the mentally challenged.

My brother will spend the rest of his life in prison. But Ted's life wasn't spared because he's any sicker than one hundred or so seriously mentally ill people that our government has executed since 1992. His life was spared because he had great lawyers.

It's probably an empty exercise to debate whether capital punishment is ever justified. Reasonable people can disagree about this philosophical question. But no reasonable person who truly understands how the current system works can, in my opinion, claim that it

> represents justice. Who lives and who dies should not depend on one's wealth, one's given mental ability, one's ethnicity or race, or the agenda of some powerful politician.

Where Things Become Fuzzy

The challenge of determining when a person has the ability to understand or appreciate the nature of his punishment is most apparent in two instances: when the Court deals with individuals of diminished mental capacity and juveniles. Here are examples of each.

Diminished Mental Capacity: The Story of Alvin Bernard Ford

Alvin Bernard Ford was convicted of murder in 1974 and sentenced to death. At no point was there evidence or any indication whatsoever that he was anything other than fully competent. However, in 1982, his behavior started to change. He became obsessed with the Ku Klux Klan, and his personal letters referenced his "Klan work" and the delusion that he was part of a Klan conspiracy designed to force him to commit suicide. This evolved into an imagined hostage crisis that included 135 friends and family members who were being held in prison.

In 1983, Ford wrote to the Florida Attorney General explaining that he, personally, had ended the crisis. He also began referring to himself as "Pope John Paul, III," and claimed responsibility for appointing a new Florida Supreme Court. Ford believed that he would not be put to death because he owned the prisons and could control the government through mind waves. He cited the landmark (and obviously non-existent) case of Ford v. State that prevented executions. His mental state continued to diminish until he was reduced to speaking in code, using the word "one" repetitively in statements like, "Hands one, face one, Mafia one, God one, father one, Pope one, Pope one, Leader one."

During this time a psychiatrist was evaluating Ford's deteriorating mental condition. The doctor, later replaced because Ford believed he was part of the conspiracy, concluded that Ford had a mental disease akin to paranoid schizophrenia. A second doctor determined that Ford lacked any understanding of his situation, and that there was no reasonable possibility that Ford was faking his condition.

Florida law required that three psychiatrists make an independent evaluation of a condemned inmate in order to determine whether he has "the mental capacity to understand the nature of the death penalty and the reasons why it was imposed upon him." In order to comply with the law, each of the three doctors met with Ford for a thirty-minute appointment. All three diagnosed Ford's mental condition differently, but they all agreed that he met this requirement.

On April 30, 1984, the Governor of Florida signed a death warrant for Ford's execution. Two years later the Supreme Court determined that the Eighth Amendment forbids putting insane people, including Alvin Ford, to death. Alvin Ford died in prison of natural causes in 1991 at the age of thirty-seven.

Juveniles: The Case of Christopher Simmons

Christopher Simmons was a seventeen-year-old in his junior year of high school when he brutally murdered a neighbor. Prior to the event, Simmons had laid out his plan to two younger friends: break into a house, tie up a victim, and throw him from a bridge. He assured his friends that they could get away with it because they were minors.

At about 2 a.m., Simmons and his accomplice–the third member wisely dropped out–went through Shirley Crook's open window and into her bedroom. The two duct-taped her eyes, mouth, and hands and drove her to a park next to a river. They reinforced her bindings, covered her head with a towel, and walked her to a railroad bridge. After tying her hands and feet together with electrical wire, they wrapped her face in duct tape and threw her over the side. Mrs. Crook drowned in the river.

Simmons bragged to friends about the killing and the police quickly arrested him. After waiving his right to an attorney, Simmons confessed to the murder and agreed to allow the police to videotape a reenactment of the crime. The State of Missouri charged Simmons with burglary, kidnapping, stealing, and murder in the first degree. Because he was seventeen at the time of the crime and could no longer be tried as a juvenile under Missouri law, he was tried as an adult. His confession, the video reenactment, and witness testimony were so compelling that no witnesses were called in his defense. The jury convicted him of murder. The jury convicted him of murder, and the State sought the death penalty.

In 2005, while Simmons's case was on appeal, the U.S. Supreme Court ruled that the Eighth Amendment forbids putting sixteen- and seventeen-year-olds to death. Based on that ruling, the State of Missouri re-sentenced Simmons to life in prison without the possibility of parole.

Conclusion

The death penalty clearly has historical roots. Despite this, there are challenging questions around the moral implications of putting humans to death. As you think about, and hopefully discuss, these questions, consider how society (and the Supreme Court) should deal with the broader issue of death. Abortion raises the issue. Stem cell research raises the issue. Physician-assisted suicide raises the issue. And, here, the death penalty does as well. Is it important to have a consistent view across the board? Are there instances in which death can be applied in a moral or ethical manner consistent with a civilized society? Or should we never promote any end that involves bringing about the death of another human being?

Footnote

At the time of editing this chapter, a Florida inmate was put to death using lethal injection. The process usually takes about fifteen minutes and includes three injections, the first to sedate the patient and the other two to kill him. In the case of Angel Diaz, it took thirty-four minutes, as the injections missed the vein and needed to be re-administered. As a result, Mr. Diaz appeared to be moving twenty-four minutes after the injections–when sedation usually occurs within three to four minutes. Florida Governor Jeb Bush immediately suspended executions using lethal injection and appointed a commission to review whether this method meets with the requirements of the Eighth Amendment. Look for developments on the web at whywellwin.com regarding this issue.

ESSAY

Marc Racicot

Former Governor, Montana

The criminal law does not punish in order to inflict suffering. It does not seek to redress violence with violence. It uses punishment to prevent the repetition of crimes. Providing for the ultimate sanction, namely the death penalty, is in my view and by any measure within the authority of a free and moral people. In Montana, where I served as Governor for eight years, death penalty legislation has been carefully and meticulously crafted, and it has been thoughtfully and rarely applied when the unequal atrocity of an offense required it.

There is no depreciation of human dignity when a criminal is rightly convicted and punished. It is a demonstration that we haven't lost confidence in our understanding of right and wrong, a shared understanding that serves as the essential glue of any civilized society. It is not the justice we are called upon to dispense that condemns the guilty man. It is his own voluntary and damning guilt that does so. He weighed what he desired against life itself, and he chose what he wanted. The enforcement of the criminal law promotes respect for that which should be respected, especially the innocent lives of others, and every crime that goes unpunished in accordance with the law takes away from the safety and security of every other person's life.

I have spent two and a half decades thinking in serious fashion about this particular issue. As a prosecutor, I tried many cases that had the potential for a death penalty to be imposed. I would have to confess that working in that arena and advocating that cause was a great deal more distant to me than considering an application for clemency and making a decision that could result in the taking of another person's life.

My own personal view is that a moral society can carefully delineate in which circumstances the death penalty should be imposed. In fact, a moral people could choose a different course that does not involve the imposition of an ultimate sanction. If it could be guaranteed, absolutely, that a murderer who has taken the life of another with deliberation would be confined for the remainder of his or her natural life with absolutely no possibility of parole, that would be, in my judgment, an acceptable course for a moral society to pursue. In fact it may even be my choice, but I do not believe that it is immoral for us as a society, in carefully circumscribed situations, to rarely impose the death penalty.

Another critical part of my thoughtful consideration of this issue arises as a result of my Catholic faith and my spiritual beliefs. I am engaged in public service largely, I believe almost exclusively, because of my faith. It stems from what I learned at the elbow of my father and mother, and the teachings I received growing up in the Catholic faith believing that there was a responsibility to give back in terms of effort or time or treasure or talent if you had it. I was taught that we need to be engaged in being of service, and that's why I set about to try and be engaged in my community in the ways that I have. That's why I sought political office. My spiritual beliefs are absolutely essential to me, and acting in concert with them is absolutely critical to my peace of mind. I recognize that I have a temporal responsibility to comply with the law, and I took an oath to comply with the law as it is, not as I would have it be. I have defended that position at every point in time to make certain that I vindicate the imperatives of the law regardless of whether or not I happen to agree. I have never found an inconsistency between my beliefs and the law such that I had to choose. As a consequence of that, the performance of my responsibilities as related to the death penalty, although searing and although I would seek at every possible opportunity to avoid it, have been consistent.

My typical approach to virtually any issue is to listen, and then to study as hard as I possibly can to learn all that I possibly can about a given issue. So, naturally, when I finally understood that these issues would be presented to me in real life terms, the first thing I did was to read the catechism of the Catholic faith. What I found is that in the Pope's Encyclical, the gospel of life, he provides for the following: it is clear that for these purposes to be achieved the nature and extent of the punishment must be carefully evaluated and decided upon and ought not to go to the extreme of executing the offender except in cases of absolute necessity. In other words, when it would not be possible otherwise to defend society.

I recognize that there are differing views, which I deeply respect. I also recognize that I am imperfect in my own capabilities, and that I need to constantly be exposed to new opportunities to learn and to grow. As a consequence of that, I am grateful for this dialogue. My great hope is that we can continue to have thoughtful and civil discussions about such searing issues in order to allow for all of us in a civilized and thoughtful and spiritual fashion to come to the right conclusion about these very, very perplexing issues. So, with that, perhaps we can have a conversation, rather than a one-sided presentation.

After many speeches and writings on this topic, some phrases may have unintentionally been used without attribution.

INDEX

T

U

About the Author

Malcolm Friedberg is the Chief Marketing Officer for a Silicon Valley company. In 2006, with a full-time position as a marketing executive, he graduated from Loyola Law School's evening program. He is currently licensed to practice law in California. Friedberg lives in Northern California with his wife and two sons.